Skelmersdale A New Town in the Making

Part One: From Fantasy to First Brick

Carol Fenlon

First published by Beacon Press

111 Blaguegate Lane
Skelmersdale
Lancashire WN8 8TY

Printed by

Flexipress, Windmill Avenue, Ormskirk L39 4QB.

A full CIP record for this book is available from the British Library

ISBN 978 0 9561059 4 3

Cover image © David Baker 2014

Acknowledgements

When I first set out to write this history I had hoped to publish the entire story of the new town in one volume. However, four years down the line, I have decided to publish the work I've completed so far to coincide with the 50th anniversary of the first brick of the new town being laid back in June 1964. Along the way many people have shared their information and stories with me. I thought I knew a lot about Skelmersdale before I started but I have learned so much more. I can't claim to be an original Skemmer; I'm originally from the Midlands and arrived in Skem in 1978 after living in Liverpool for 12 years but I have loved the town since I first set eyes on it and hope this entitles me to make this attempt at chronicling its recent history. My thanks go to all the people who have talked to me about their experiences of living here. If their information is not in this volume, it will be in the next.

Special thanks must go to Norman Lyon for his memories of life during the designation period; to Charlie Denton for his observations on the politics of the new town proposals and to William Waterworth for his accounts of farming life and the upheaval caused to Skelmersdale farmers by the advent of the new town. Thanks also to Andrew Brown, editor of the Ormskirk Advertiser group for permission to use extracts and photos from past issues.

Thanks go to William Waterworth for providing photographs of Skelmersdale in pre-new town times; to David Baker and Harold Swift for generous assistance with photographs to illustrate this volume and to David Ball of the Glassball Project (www.glassball.org) for sharing images of Skelmersdale and also for his continued encouragement and sharing of resources.

I am indebted to Marianne Howell of Lancashire libraries for endless advice on the history of Skelmersdale and also to Harold Swift for his help in identifying long lost names and places. I must also give grateful thanks to Mike Pearson for advice on the history of philanthropic villages and garden cities and all three have been instrumental in advising on content and correcting my mistakes.

Finally a word of thanks to Flexipress printers of Ormskirk who patiently helped with cover design and layout, to members of Skelmersdale Writers' Group who have kept me writing through thick and thin and to all the people of Skelmersdale for making our town worth writing about.

Carol Fenlon has lived in Skelmersdale for over thirty years. She came to Skelmersdale from Liverpool in 1978 and has since taken a keen interest in the history of both the old and the new town.

She is also a novelist and short story writer and much of her fiction is set in West Lancashire. Her first novel, *Consider the Lilies,* won the Impress Novel Prize 2007.

Read extracts of her work at www.carolfenlon.com

Contents

Chapter One: Before the New Town

In this chapter I intend only to give a brief outline of the history of Skelmersdale before its development as a new town in the mid-twentieth century. This is because several excellent accounts and memoirs of Skelmersdale before it became a new town already exist and the main focus of this work is on the new town development. It is, however, necessary to locate the new town of Skelmersdale in relation to the old town it engulfed in order to understand the reasons for its designation as a new town and in order to fully explore the relationship between old and new Skemmers.

There is no mention of Skelmersdale in the sketchy records of early Britain. The land between the rivers Ribble and Mersey consisted of swamp and thick forests where dangerous animals roamed, not an attractive site for settlement.

Nevertheless, in the first century A.D. Roman legions arrived in Lancashire to subdue the native iron age Brigantes who had settlements in the area. Iron was mined at Wigan during this early period and some roads had been made to enable passage between Lancaster, Chester and York but significant settlement did not occur until the advent of groups of Angles from the North East of England in the sixth century A.D. (Bagley, 1976).

In the ninth century A.D. Norsemen began to invade and settle the area and it is likely that one of these gave his name to the settlement of Skelmersdale. Various spellings of the name occur from this period on; Schelmeresdale, Skelmersden, Skialdmarr (Ekwall 1972) and Skjalmaar (Mills 1976) to name a few. The usual interpretation is that the first part Skelmer refers to the name of a Norseman who settled there, thus Skelmer's dale or valley.

Part of Domesday map showing Lancashire and Skelmersdale.

The first real record of the existence of Skelmersdale comes in the 11th century Domesday Book where Schelmeresdale is recorded as being one carucate of land held by Uctred valued for tax at thirty two pence, within the area known as the West Derby Hundred or Wapentake, which was held by Roger of Poitou as a reward from William I after the Norman Conquest. Uctred also held the nearby manors of Achetun (Aughton) and Lathom (Baines1870).

In 1137 the West Derby Hundred, of which Skelmersdale was part, passed to William Earl of Derby by his marriage to Agnes, sister of Ranulf de Blundeville and the long association of the area with the earls of Derby began.

By this time the district had at least on the surface become completely Christian and many churches were built. As in the rest of Britain, political machinations between the Church and increasingly powerful lords and landowners characterised the medieval period, particularly in the areas of Lathom and Upholland (Bagley, ibid). Whether such power struggles and intrigues touched the lives of people in Skelmersdale we do not know but it seems unlikely. Skelmersdale remained a tiny settlement and for most of its history was a satellite village of the burgeoning town of Ormskirk (Padfield 1986).

We might imagine that the inhabitants of Skelmersdale would have been kept too busy scraping a living from the land, warding off marauding wild animals and coping with occasional outbreaks of plague, to take much notice of the passage of lords and ladies to nearby Lathom House and Upholland. Edward II stayed at Upholland Priory in 1323 and Eyre (1976) reports that kings crossed the Tawd bridge at Upholland on the way to Lathom House for five centuries from 1189 until 1643.

What kind of living the villagers could have made can only be imagined. It must have been hard going as the moss land was so waterlogged at this time that it could not be worked. Travel too was fraught with difficulty on the boggy land and through thickly forested areas. Centuries later Oliver Cromwell would describe the road from Preston to Wigan as, 'twelve miles of such ground as I never rode in all my life,'(Bagley, 1976:88).

Nevertheless, despite its minor status, Skelmersdale would surely have been caught up in the fever of political intrigue and religious foment that culminated in the 17th century civil war and the Reformation.

In 1642 royalist troops were mustered near Ormskirk and Lathom was a hotspot of activity, being the seat of the fiercely royalist Earl of Derby. The Earl headed forces intent on conquering towns in Lancashire and the Midlands on behalf of the deposed king, Charles I. Normal life floundered as pitched battles continued all over Lancashire, where hundreds were slain at a time.

The siege of Lathom House by the Parliamentarians, taking place in 1644 and again in 1645 could not have failed to impact on the village of Skelmersdale so close by. Although Charlotte de Tremouille, the loyal Countess of Derby, successfully defended the castle against the first attack of Parliamentarians during her husband's absence, the tide turned inexorably against the Royalists and by 1645 Lathom House stood virtually alone as their stronghold. It succumbed to a second siege in July 1645 and represented such a significant victory that thanksgivings were ordered in London and Westminster (Baines 1870). Derby fought on for several years from a base in the Isle of Man and his final march passed through Upholland and therefore probably, Skelmersdale, on the way to the battle of Wigan Lane where he was defeated and captured. Lathom House was razed to the ground in symbolic retribution. James, the seventh earl of Derby, was executed in October 1651 and all his property seized, including the village of Skelmersdale.

A representation of Lathom House, original seat of the Earls of Derby, near Skelmersdale which was razed to the ground in the English Civil War.

Skelmersdale then passed through various hands. It was sold to Thomas Ashurst of Dalton in 1717, then sold on to Sir Thomas Bootle of Lathom in 1751, eventually passing to Edward Bootle Wilbraham, second Lord Skelmersdale, who became Earl of Lathom in 1880 (Eyre,1976).

Little is known of life in Skelmersdale before 1800 but we may imagine that the village was a typical small agricultural community that lay in the shadow of the thriving town of Ormskirk. The aforementioned Thomas Ashurst provided it with a school in 1732. In 1801 a census showed the population of Skelmersdale as being 414 (Molyneux, 1981) but the burgeoning industrial revolution and its voracious appetite for coal was about to burst onto the scene, bringing with it the development that would make Skelmersdale into a town in its own right.

Prior to the eighteenth century, coal had little value, at first picked up in small amounts on beaches as 'sea-coal' and later mined by individuals or small groups in shallow bell-shaped pits. However, rapid population growth and industrial development throughout the eighteenth century generated an increasing demand for fuel and coal soon came to be seen as the only significant source of energy. Howell (2010) notes that the account books of Richard Lathom list an item for 16 baskets of coal in 1727, around the same time that potato growing, the other great mainstay of Lancashire, was introduced.   On the

1839 tithe map of Skelmersdale, 22 field names which include the word 'pit' bear witness to the growing interest in coal, although the label 'pit' also referred to marl pits and depressions where pools formed.

With the advance of the industrial revolution and the invention of the steam engine, the rapid acceleration of factory production and the concentration of population in towns and cities required supplies of industrial and domestic coal on a scale never before seen. Although the existence of coal in Skelmersdale was well known, its development as a mining area was late in comparison to other Lancashire coalfields such as Wigan. In the early nineteenth century, Skelmersdale remained an agricultural community, its industry centred around cornmills and quarries (Sands 1970) and in 1851, 75% of workers migrating to Skelmersdale were employed in agriculture (Molyneux ibid).

Molyneux argues that the major factor responsible for the rapid establishment of Skelmersdale as a mining town was the arrival of the railway.

An original Grosvenor series postcard in the author's collection.

This enabled efficient transport of coal and easier immigration of workers from other coalmining areas. As a result, mining developed rapidly and the population jumped from 414 in 1801 to 6,627 in 1891 (Molyneux ibid). Prior to the 1850s, stagecoaches ran from Wigan to Ormskirk and from Manchester to Southport. Coal had to be taken by horse-drawn wagons either to the cities or to the Leeds-Liverpool canal.

The main Lancashire-Yorkshire railway line from Ormskirk to St Helens arrived in Skelmersdale in March 1858 and subsidiary mineral branch lines soon developed, connecting the new collieries to the main line. Sands (2008) lists twenty five pits in the Skelmersdale area, operating at various times between 1840 and 1940 while Skelmersdale Heritage Society (2007) puts the figure at forty four collieries in and around Skelmersdale.

The railway also facilitated the immigration of miners from other areas. Although Molyneux's figures (1981) show that most miners came from the immediate areas of Wigan and Bickerstaffe, a significant number came from further afield, from Scottish, South Welsh, Derbyshire, Staffordshire and North East coalfields. Their legacy can still be seen in the street names of Old Skelmersdale, such as Stafford Street, Durham Street and Cardiff Street. One wonders if the miners from these areas segregated themselves in specific streets as new houses sprang up around Sandy Lane and Stormy Corner to accommodate the influx.

Blaguegate Colliery: Photo courtesy of Harold Swift.

This new housing development and its ancillary complement of shops and services laid the foundation for Skelmersdale's identity as an urban centre, eclipsing its former status as a rural village clinging to the skirts of Ormskirk.

Molyneux (ibid) identifies four major landowners in Skelmersdale in 1854; Lord Skelmersdale, Richard Prescott, James Culshaw and Thomas Brandreth, but it was small, local landowners who provided quickly built, cheap housing for the working population. Despite the formation of a local council and committee board to govern the town from 1874, which later became the Urban District Council in 1894, there was little in the way of housing control or public health regulation.

The influx of miners and other workers into Skelmersdale, not only increased the population but dramatically altered its structure. In 1841, 29% of the population was aged between 20 and 50 but this figure grew to 42% by 1901 (Molyneux ibid), giving the town a youthful vibrancy.

By the 1870s there was a network of services in place to minister to the 'new town' development. Churches were built to cater to the variety of denominations present, including a Welsh Chapel. St Richard's Catholic church opened in 1865. A school board was formed in 1878 to address the problem of insufficient school places and piped water was laid on in 1874. In 1878 the town acquired a gasworks, built on land near the proposed new road to be named Clayton Street. A gas and water committee was set up to oversee the service and also dealt with problems and minor misdemeanours. In its early days two boys caught damaging street lamps were brought before the committee by the local constabulary, but were let off when their grandmothers appeared to plead for them (Harris 1956).

T. W. Riseley, 32, LIVERPOOL ROAD, SKELMERSDALE.

Who is this gentleman – a miner dressed in his Sunday best or a merchant offering goods or services? The latter would seem more likely seeing as the photograph includes his name and address. A photo from the author's collection.

The sudden growth of the town was not all progress, however. On the downside, the increase in population and industrial development meant overcrowding for some, and exposure to hazards and disease. Figures for childhood diseases, accidents and fatalities all increased. In his introduction to the 1907 map of Skelmersdale, Godfrey (2001) argues, 'the exploitation of coal was a very mixed blessing for this previously unremarkable and secluded location,' as little of the profit from coal found its way back into the community. By the 1890s, subsidence caused by mining was endemic, to the point that the Chapel of Ease, precursor to the church of St Paul became unsafe for public use in 1897. A report in the Lancet of 1874, describes conditions found in Skelmersdale. 'The houses, many of the most miserable construction, are almost buried in the filth of the inhabitants. The privies, so foul as to repel even those most familiarised with them. The drainage accumulated in horrible puddles, fed also by the liquid abominations of pigsties and middensteads' (quoted in Orr 2005:7). Yet the town had a thriving social life with plenty of pubs and two brass bands, the Old Prize band formed in 1874 and the Temperance band formed in 1883. Skelmersdale United football team was founded in 1882 and became the district's premier club in the 1890s, paving the way for a multitude of teams in the Ormskirk and District Amateur League in the early twentieth century (Malia, undated, early 2000s?).

MISSION CHURCH. SKELMERSDALE. 13

Skelmersdale mission church, an original postcard by Hutchinson; from the author's collection.

For immigrants from heavily industrialised landscapes, such as Thomas Yates, a child of a mine manager, whose family moved to Skelmersdale from Abram, near Wigan in 1907, the open countryside of Skelmersdale provided welcome relief from the rigours of the coalface. Yates (undated c.1976) describes a lifestyle which must have been common for Skelmersdale miners, where time was divided between lucrative work down the pit and the tending of gardens, rented land or smallholdings to provide food and perhaps a secondary, more pleasurable source of income.

This rapid period of growth was shortlived. By the mid 1890s coal mining had passed its peak and the Tawd Vale colliery disaster of

1897sounded the death knell for the town's mining industry. On the 30th November 1897, the Tawd river burst its banks after torrential rain and flooded into the Tawd Vale shaft where it met an underground fire which had been burning for many years. The resulting explosion of steam wrecked the pit which closed for several years, to be re-opened as Glenburn colliery in the early twentieth century. Although the explosion claimed only two lives as it occurred after most of the miners had left for the day, it was a disaster for the town, causing massive unemployment and the immediate exodus of almost 50% of the working population (Molyneux 1981), an economic collapse which eerily presages events that were to take place in the new town in the late 1970s.

Whitemoss colliery rescue squad from an original postcard in the author's collection

Even as the newly industrialised Victorian town of Skelmersdale was still consolidating the development of its services and social structure, the decline of the mining industry which had created the town put the community on a gradual path towards dereliction which by the mid-twentieth century made it a prime choice for regeneration under the postwar British New Towns policy.

By 1901, the town population had dropped from its 1890s peak of 6,627 to 5,699 (Sands 1970). Despite the introduction of expensive machinery such as the Driscoll Disc cutting machine at Glenburn colliery around 1910, miners such as Thomas Yates found themselves forced to travel to Cronton colliery to get work as, one by one, the Skelmersdale pits closed down, so that by 1938 only 12 pits remained (Orr 2005). The decline that began with the Tawd Vale disaster was accelerated by national events including the devastation of the Great War and the strikes and economic depressions of the 1920s and 30s. Despite poverty and unemployment following the coal strikes of 1921 and the General Strike of 1926, Sandy Lane had consolidated itself as the economic centre of Skelmersdale, taking precedence over the earlier settlement of Stormy Corner.

Earlier, 1895 had seen the establishment of the Co-operative Society on the High Street, although it later moved to Witham Road. It is not clear when the Market Hall was built at the junction of the High Street and Sandy Lane, but it is mentioned in reports of the Rose Farm murder case of 1901. A bank was opened in Sandy Lane in 1920, and the Town Hall and Coronation Park were both nearby. Mary Cuckson (1997) records there being 46 shops in Sandy Lane in the 1920s and 30s.

A postcard sent to William Ashcroft in 1933 at the cottage hospital in Holywell, Flintshire, from his mother. It shows how neat Coronation Park was and also shows the rows of mining cottages, a few of which still survive today off Witham Road and Sandy Lane. (Postcard from the author's collection).

In spite of economic difficulties between the two world wars, Skelmersdale people enjoyed a well developed social life, reminiscent of many large villages and small semi- rural towns. After the old market hall was taken over by the Skelmersdale Shoe company in 1919, dances were held in the Sunday School Mission hall, the Masonic hall and the Town hall, until the purpose built Majestic ballroom opened in the early 1930s to the delight of local residents (Cuckson, ibid). Local bands: Doris Draper's, Harry Simms' and Bill Gregson's, played the nights away and for several months Eric Norman's repertory troupe produced plays in the Majestic. The Majestic later became a cinema, competing with Billy Shaw's Empire Picture Palace, before eventually becoming Skelmersdale Labour Club.

Both Cuckson and Rigby (in Hodges c.1996) recall Charlie Bailey's ice cream, while Thomas Yates sings the praises of his tripe and chips and mentions Charlie Mason's Dandelion and Burdock. Charlie Mason's lemonade and ginger beer bottles still turn up occasionally at local car boot sales and auctions.

Although the railway brought improved transport and widened the horizons of the population, the rural aspect of Skelmersdale continued to influence social life. Rural walks and pastimes remained popular. Both Cuckson and Rigby (ibid) recall the walking days and subsequent tea-parties held by each church's Sunday school every summer. These were major events, attended by all ages, the elderly being provided with horse-drawn landaus to transport them with the procession to the relevant church hall, where a splendid tea was provided, followed by games and dancing, and in Mary Cuckson's case, the delights of Silcock's fair which would be ensconced on the neighbouring playing field.

Various Charlie Mason bottles from the author's collection

These authors, writing of their youth and looking back on halcyon days, seemed unaware of the terrible uncertainty that hung over the future of Skelmersdale, at the levels of regional and national decision making. Since the beginning of the twentieth century, awareness had been growing at national level of the problems of unchecked urban development. Lack of specific planning policies in previous centuries, and particularly in Victorian times, had resulted in a hotchpotch of residential and industrial development, forming into huge cities that swallowed up smaller towns and villages by ribbon development along major roads.

From the turn of the century, town and country planning was advocated as a means of controlling future development and the ramifications of this would affect the far flung villages and towns on the peripheries of large cities like Liverpool.

A report of the South West Lancashire Joint Town Planning Advisory Committee, produced in 1930, discussed the future development of South West Lancashire, identifying Liverpool as of central importance in the regional plan.

At government level various suggestions for alleviating congestion in inner cities, were being considered. These included the provision of satellite towns linked to the major city and the provision of industrial or trading estates away from residential areas. The garden city or new town, along the lines of Ebenezer Howard's Letchworth or Welwyn, was also something discussed as a possible national policy. Howard's philosophy will be discussed in detail in the next chapter but suffice it to say here that the first garden cities, Letchworth and Welwyn, were created by private enterprise at the beginning of the twentieth century, realising Howard's vision of self-sufficient, healthy communities. Howard's ideas greatly influenced the development of the British post-war new towns policy.

The Heritage museum at Letchworth in Hertfordshire, Ebenezer Howard's first garden city.

The advisory committee report discussed declining industry in the South West Lancashire region, and identified Ormskirk as a possible dormitory town for Liverpool. It focused on the need for the regeneration of industry in the area but rather than selecting an area where need was highest such as in Skelmersdale, it recommended Burscough as the best site for redevelopment because of its excellent transport facilities as it boasted good road, rail and waterway links.

The future of Skelmersdale was discussed in several parts of the report. It noted the town's industrial profile as mostly light industry with a predominance of female employees working in the rope works, the shoe factory and the cotton mill. The majority of Skelmersdale men were employed in mining yet the report stated that the Skelmersdale coal seams were expected to be exhausted by 1940. There was little enthusiasm for the future development of Skelmersdale and few strategies were identified for rectifying the employment situation. The word 'dying' was used several times and the main impression gained is that Skelmersdale was considered to be something of a hopeless case.

The report concluded in favour of creating a whole ring of satellite towns to circle Liverpool and relieve congestion of the city. Areas were identified along the north coast of Merseyside, Ormskirk and St Helens and along the south coast of Liverpool. Locations suggested for satellite development were Speke, Hale, Halewood, Knowsley, Kirkby, Maghull and Hightown.

All these new developments were to be zoned into agricultural, industrial, residential and commercial areas and this policy was to be extended to the development of existing communities such as Ormskirk and Town Green, Burscough and Rainford.

Doubt was again expressed about any development for Skelmersdale, so that it was virtually left out of the plan, apart from some zoning along the railway line for industrial development and a half-hearted suggestion that the town might be developed as a dormitory for St Helens. In effect Skelmersdale was expected to fade away and die a quiet and unremarkable death in the overall scheme for West Lancashire.

Perhaps fortunately for Skelmersdale, the report was only advisory in nature – making recommendations to local authorities to assist them in formulating their plans for their areas. In the depressed circumstances of the nineteen-thirties and the build up to the second world war, development slowed and at the outbreak of hostilities in September 1939 virtually all plans went on hold as the country united in the war effort.

At the beginning of 1939, although war had not yet been certain, there was an air of inevitability and the local press was already reporting plans for the evacuation of children from Liverpool, emergency transport and blackout regulations.

In February 1939 the first roundabout in Skelmersdale was proposed at a meeting of Skelmersdale Council, to be sited at the junction of Four Lane Ends and a new road planned to run to the Fox and Goose at Tawd Bridge. However, in view of the economic situation, it was felt there was not much chance of it actually being built in the near future, one councillor remarking that, "the County seems to leave Skelmersdale behind" (Ormskirk Advertiser 16.2.39).

The month before, the directors of White Moss Colliery had voted to close the mine. This caused questions in Parliament over the loss of 500 jobs in a town already blighted by unemployment. It had been hoped that the building of the proposed new road would provide much needed jobs for the townspeople.

Whitemoss Colliery, photo by kind permission of Harold Swift. The colliery stood close to the site where Scott Rees & Co. Solicitors stands today on Gardiners Place.

At this same council meeting, a proposal was put forward to open a community centre where the unemployed of Skelmersdale could be trained in 'interesting occupations.' The chairman commented, "It is an effort to find the men something to do, rather than have them standing at the street corners."

Ormskirk's MP investigated the possibility of government assistance to keep White Moss colliery open and also to create new industries in Skelmersdale but his proposals were declined as the town was not a Special Area within the meaning of the Special Areas Act of 1934.

In March 1939, Skelmersdale was suggested as the possible site of a potato processing factory but this seemed to be clutching at straws. Ormskirk employment exchange reported 503 persons registered as unemployed that month, approximately 10% of the total population although pea-picking and potato harvesting was expected to provide some relief in the summer months (Ormskirk Advertiser, 23.3.39).

Housing was another major problem in Skelmersdale at this time. The 1930 report noted that in 1921, 20% of the town's population was overcrowded, a higher percentage than Liverpool and only surpassed in the entire region by St Helens. In February 1939, Ormskirk Rural District Council discussed the high price of sites for rural housing and expressed concern about the state of existing housing in the district

(Ormskirk Advertiser 9.2.39). Only fifteen new houses were built in Skelmersdale in 1938 but the Medical Officer of Health reported that there was less overcrowding as people were leaving the town in search of work elsewhere.

Despite these problems and the looming threat of war, Skelmersdale people continued their annual activities as normal. Skelmersdale Football Club won the Liverpool Challenge Cup and Lillian Powell of Clayton Street was elected Miss Skelmersdale at a social in the Skelmersdale Arms (Ormskirk Advertiser 27.4.39). Darts, bowling and billiards continued to be popular and the Birkdale Players performed at the Congregational School. Children's school tea-parties and church walking days were as prolific as ever. Children from the Methodist Sunday school on the High Street went by train for a day out to Southport and those from the Methodist School went to Kent on a camping holiday that included a trip to London (Ormskirk Advertiser 27.7.39). At this time there was no senior school in Skelmersdale, although fundraising efforts were afoot to provide a Roman Catholic senior school and Lancashire County Council received petitions regarding the provision of a state senior school for the town.

The Skelmersdale Shoe Company had a sports festival and at the Skelmersdale Council School sports day, Councillor Farrimond, Chairman of the Skelmersdale Urban District Council, declared that Skelmersdale children were the nicest in the world (Ormskirk Advertiser : ibid.) Two hundred and twenty people went in seven coaches on Ted Draper's trip to Blackpool and the Skelmersdale carnival was held in August as usual.

Digmoor C.E Sunday School Class on their walking day c. 1939.
Picture by kind permission of Harold Swift.

The declaration of war in September 1939, however, had immediate effects on the local as well as national economy. Almost immediately the potato crop and bacon supplies were requisitioned by the government. The call-up of able-bodied men resulted in a shortage of agricultural labour, which, although going someway to alleviate the unemployment problem, created new difficulties in working the land.

In the first week of the war, 3,500 children were evacuated from Merseyside into the West Lancashire area. Two trainloads of children arrived at Skelmersdale and many thanks were recorded from Liverpool families to Skelmersdale people who, "opened their homes and their hearts to receive the children," (Ormskirk Advertiser 12.10.39). In fact despite a steady trickle of evacuees returning to Liverpool in other districts, Skelmersdale retained most of their allocation, due to the welcome given to the children by the people (Ormskirk Advertiser 23.11.39).

The winter of 1939-1940 was a bad one with many roads blocked by snow. Skelmersdale, Stormy and Digmoor were completely cut off for over a week. Unemployment still dogged Skelmersdale. Despite the call-up and new government contracts, the wartime restrictions on transport created further difficulties. The promised potato factory opened in February and in August a glass plant started up. An egg-packing station commenced production in October, but these were fairly small operations and the privations of war were already beginning to bite deep.

The town suffered its first war death with the loss of Gunner Harry Fairclough of the Royal Field Artillery. There was no Skelmersdale carnival and Ted Draper's annual trip was cancelled. Skelmersdale United hoped to carry on playing but had to suspend games for the duration in October. Public shelters were erected as bombings were reported over Merseyside and areas of Lancashire. There was a hosepipe ban and blackout regulations were strictly enforced.

On a cheerier note the Ormskirk Advertiser (31.10.40) reported that the postwar function of the new Ministry of Town Works and Buildings would be to rebuild town and country, but then who was to know that the war would drag on for another five years?

In the same year of 1940, a Royal Commission examined 'The Distribution of the Industrial Population', commonly known as the Barlow Report. It took up and developed further, ideas proposed in the earlier regional South West Lancashire Joint Advisory Committee report, in a recommended national policy for urban development based on the creation of garden cities, or garden suburbs, satellite towns, trading estates and the expansion of existing small towns. This report will be discussed in greater detail in the next chapter. We note its publication here at a time when the necessities of war prevented its implementation. However, by the beginning of 1945, the end was in sight. Both the regional and national presses were full of optimistic plans for the future, for re-building battered Britain and revitalising its long-suffering population, under the guiding light of a new and enthusiastic Labour government. Skelmersdale, now designated as a Development Area, teetered on the brink of a new and totally unexpected future.

Chapter Two

British New Towns Policy: Vision and Reality

How did the concept of the new town arise? In 1946 the New Towns Act consolidated proposals to create new towns across Britain as the answer to inner city congestion and decay. The inner city problem had been growing for over a century but the devastation caused by Germany's attacks on Britain's major cities meant that the issue could no longer be ignored. The new post-war Labour government was inspired by visions of a new and better, modern society yet the idea of the new town was not a recent phenomenon. It incorporated aspects of Victorian so-called philanthropic planned villages, early twentieth-century garden cities and satellite towns. These very real communities themselves contained elements of mythical utopias and ideal cities which were in circulation in Britain from medieval times and probably had been present since cities first began to develop into amorphous masses.

In this chapter I will attempt to identify and trace the development of these strands and discuss the philosophical ideas involved and their interpretation in the light of the realities of economic and political trends. By this means we may understand the post-war British New Towns policy and at a more personal level, see how and why Skelmersdale came to be chosen as a new town site.

Left to themselves, without urban planning, cities have historically developed in higgledy-piggledy disorder. Living entities, they swell and grow, their centres becoming increasingly overcrowded and insanitary. Their inhabitants, flocking in from the countryside to share in the prosperity of the great metropolis, find themselves stressed, often impoverished and prone to the diseases that flourish in the congested centres. In many ancient cities such as Istanbul, these congested quarters can still be found, where unwary travellers may soon become lost in a labyrinth of narrow streets and crumbling buildings which are perpetually filled with crowded humanity.

Social institutions also develop with the city's expansion. They grow, reach their peak, become rigid and slide into decadence, mirroring the concrete existence of the city. From early times, dissatisfaction with civilised life, with the policies and practices of church, state, monarchy and government, surfaced in tales of mythical ideal civilisations.

The story of Automathes (Kirkby, 1745), probably originated from a medieval folk-tale, but was frequently re-worked in later centuries. In fact its similarity to the original *Tarzan, Lord of the Apes* suggests it may well have informed Edgar Rice Burroughs's work. The infant Automathes, shipwrecked on a desert island, grows up, without civilised company or education, to found a society based on fairness and justice, guided by observing the designing hand of God. Such stories foreground the corruption and unfairness of existing societies and are virtually proposals for new and better civilisations. Thomas More's *Utopia* (in Bruce 1999), first published in 1516, advocates the separation of cities by at least twenty miles of land and speaks of husbandry rather than ownership of land, of a communal life without property. In More's ideal society, all would be educated in agriculture and in the safeguarding of existing knowledge. Most importantly, everyone should have a garden.

Illustration from 'Utopia' by Thomas More, published 1516.

Leonardo da Vinci also developed plans for ten cities each with five thousand homes, to be built from scratch, where pedestrians and horse traffic would be separated by gardens and municipal irrigation (Mumford in Howard, 1965).

Many of these fabrications were idealistic, as much concerned with sweeping away corruption and exploitation as with providing clean living conditions, yet remnants of these ideas can be seen in twentieth-century proposals for garden cities and new town developments: the surrounding belt of green land, plans for education and well-being, the communal ownership of the town and the emphasis on gardens and green spaces. Perhaps because of their idealism, these Renaissance plans remained firmly on paper while the cities formed in the early part of human civilisation continued to sprawl without check.

It was perhaps the advent of the Industrial Revolution that forced the issue. The increasing urbanisation of labour in city factories swelled the already overcrowded residential warrens to bursting point, while the free market forces of capitalism created huge groups of impoverished elderly and unemployed persons. In addition, due to economic trends, change was inevitable. The advent of steam power meant that industries such as spinning and weaving found it expedient to re-locate to sites with suitable climates for their products, near ample water and coal supplies, yet such locations had few facilities to cater for the social life of large numbers of workers. As people migrated to the major towns and cities in search of work, country life became increasingly impoverished. The city was not just a source of employment but also of entertainment and culture for those who could afford it. Whereas it may be argued that in earlier times, town and country had co-existed in complementary fashion, in the industrial age, they became increasingly polarised.

The first attempt to address these problems, albeit at an individual level, was the building of New Lanark by the 'enlightened' capitalists David Dale and Robert Owen in the late eighteenth century. Between 1780 and 1816, Dale built a cotton mill in the Clyde valley on the way to Glasgow, with a village to house its workforce. The mill had a fair pay policy, limited working hours and employed no child labour. The homes provided were tenements in traditional Scottish style, which may look grim to us today, but which represented a major improvement on the slums of the city.

A modern day view of New Lanark. Note the proximity to the water supply that would drive the mill and the tenement construction of the dwellings.

Owen was much influenced by the Enlightenment view that the child forms the adult and that health and education are essential to successful development. Although the motives of both Owen and Dale were undoubtedly philanthropic, in practice their ideas were paternalistic, controlling every aspect of their tenants' lives. The school provided at New Lanark was called 'The Institute for the Foundation of Character'. There were no public houses and strict rules governed the tenancies. The provision of a self-contained ready-made town provided the owners with a contented but dependent workforce, reliant on them for the very roofs over their heads as well as the bread in their mouths. Nevertheless, New Lanark was a remarkable innovation and soon became famous round the world.

In 1835 The Municipal Corporations Act established local government control for city boroughs in response to the perceived need for structured development of distinct city areas, e.g. closely packed slum housing districts and the growth of middle class suburbs. Uncontrolled, poorly constructed housing, the prevalence of disease and poor sanitary conditions were the motivations that produced early efforts in town planning (Ward, 1994).

In 1848 James Buckingham produced a plan for a model industrial town, (Mumford, ibid) and, in 1853, the town of Saltaire was built on the Leeds-Liverpool canal near Bradford by Sir Titus Salt, a wealthy mill owner and a Congregationalist with strong philanthropic ideals.

Contemporary view of Saltaire cottages

The town, built round an alpaca mill, had 775 homes and 45 alms-houses arranged in 22 streets. It contained a church, a school and an Institute in which a library, lecture theatre, gymnasium and billiard room were housed. There was also a public wash house and rules for the village residents specified that they must wash at least twice a week.

As at New Lanark, there were no public houses in Saltaire and a strict set of rules was imposed on each tenant. Sir Titus reserved the right to enter and inspect their homes at any time, yet paternalistic control was balanced by the provision of healthy living conditions. There was a company dining room where workers could buy meals cheaply or could bring their own food to be cooked while they worked and allotment gardens were provided round the outskirts of the village.

The other two major model villages, Port Sunlight in Cheshire and Bournville, near Birmingham, were also built by industrialists with strong religious convictions. Port Sunlight, built by Lord Lever to service his soap factory in the 1880s, is perhaps the most flamboyant example of the philanthropic village. Constructed to impress and demonstrate its creator's wealth and taste with no expense spared, it displays an amazing variety of architectural styles with wonderful gardens and waterways. Port Sunlight's homes all have gardens and green zoning was built into the plan, one of the first towns to be so designed.

A block of the beautiful properties Lever built at Port Sunlight.

The quality of building was superb and the town included similar facilities to Saltaire – a church and school, a theatre and a cottage hospital as well as a swimming pool and gymnasium. Despite his paternalistic stipulation that only his workers could live in the town, he did permit a public house to be built although at first this was only intended for the use of visiting soap buyers and not for the refreshment of the workforce. Lord Lever's paternalism may be described as 'liberal'. For him a deprived child became a depraved adult and everything at Port Sunlight was designed to prevent this (Sunday Times 24.12.95).

Similar principles motivated the Quaker Cadbury family to build Bournville, located next to their chocolate factory near Birmingham, also constructed in the 1880s. The design was less spectacular than that of Port Sunlight, showing a more classical Arts and Crafts influence but the provision of a healthy environment and good facilities for workers was the same. These planned communities became famous worldwide and were copied in other countries as well as by smaller manufacturers in Britain. Smaller examples include Bromborough on the Wirral peninsula, built by Price, the candle manufacturer and Springvale village near Darwen, built around a cotton mill.

A modern view of Bournville shops. It probably looked more effective in horse drawn carriage days.

These model villages were one-off experiments in Victorian philanthropy, built by capitalists with vast wealth to invest and as such represented unique efforts by individual benefactors rather than any consistent housing policy. Their creation demonstrates the attitudes and practical needs of their owners, but these criteria continued to influence future planning. Many of the characteristics of the philanthropic villages can be seen in the planning of new towns as far ahead as the 1960s, including the new town of Skelmersdale. We may summarise them as follows: 1) an emphasis on green space; 2) planned self-sufficient communities; 3) the provision of good rented housing and healthy living conditions; 4) a settled residential community forming a workforce matched to local industry; 5) insistence on tenants of good character; 6) the re-location of industry away from major city centres; 7) the siting of new residential communities not far from the periphery of a major conurbation, thus relieving inner city congestion.

The philanthropic villages also showed the beginnings of concern about the need for town and country planning, recognition of the need to control the unchecked development of market forces and to monitor their effects on the cities themselves and on the people living in them. The better off classes were not immune to the diseases that raced through the poorer quarters of the cities and governments of the late nineteenth century were concerned about social unrest in the face of growing working class militancy (Ward, 1994). Social unrest was not confined to the working classes, however. As Hall & Ward (1998) remark, London toward the end of the century had become 'a hotbed of radical activity' with many intellectuals pushing for the creation of a new society (P.6).

Housing was seen as one way of defusing this militancy without entering into the politics of the re-distribution of wealth (Ward, 1994). Street clearances of some of the worst slums in this period reduced the stock of available cheap housing, and from 1851, councils were legally able to provide municipal housing, although few did so, preferring to rely on private developers and philanthropy. The housing problem refused to disappear however, and in 1890 the Housing of the Working Class Act allowed for more extensive council house building but the numbers of properties actually built remained very small.

In 1900 a pressure group named the National Housing Reform Council was formed which originally advocated municipal housing with government finance but soon turned to support for a partnership between private and municipal development in town planning (Ward, ibid). Despite this, on a wider scale, little was done until Ebenezer Howard determined to make his dream of the 'garden city' a reality at the turn of the nineteenth century. Howard's garden cities are commonly acknowledged as the precursors of the modern new town and accordingly it is worth examining his life and work in some detail.

Ebenezer Howard's Garden City Ideal

Unlike earlier philanthropists, Ebenezer Howard had no economic agenda, nor did he have at his disposal vast resources to translate his ideas into reality. The son of a small shopkeeper in London, he worked as a clerk in England and America. However, he had a passion for inventions, although they brought him little money, and it was his flair for invention that led him to develop the concept of the garden city. (Osborn, in Howard, 1965).

Howard, then had no capitalist or political interest. Like More, centuries earlier, his primary concept of an ideal town was that of a 'socialist community' (Osborn, ibid: 21), where all would participate in the growth of the town but none would own it. Howard was much influenced by J.S Mill's *Principles of Political Economy* and U.S. writer Edward Bellamy's vision of an utopian society in Boston 2000, written in the 1880s (Hall & Ward, 1998).

At the heart of the problem, in Howard's view, was the separation of town and country caused by the industrial age and he identified various 'attractions' which drew people to and from town and country. These 'attractions' resulted in imbalances of population with corresponding social and economic difficulties. Both town and country had their advantages and disadvantages. The town offered work and high wages with the opportunity to widen personal horizons by mixing with people from different classes and different areas. The city also offered a variety of social interests and amusements. On the other hand there were problems of overcrowding, foul air and ugly surroundings with little greenery. City dwellers suffered long working hours, poor conditions and high rents; they had to travel long distances to work and there was always the potential for loneliness in the midst of a crowd. The country offered a pleasant aspect with rural pastimes but wages were low, there were few amenities and little social stimulation. With the decline of agriculture, many villages were in poor condition and work in rural districts was in short supply.

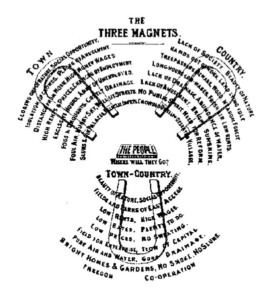

Howard's concept of the Three Magnets. The bottom one, Town-Country represents Howard's vision of the amalgamation of the two in the garden city.

These attractions and detractions caused people to flow between town and country at different periods, creating imbalance and subsequent social and economic problems. His diagram of the three magnets illustrates the attractions and disadvantages of town and country and proposes the solution 'town-country,' his dream of the 'garden city,' which would marry the attractions of both and thus neutralise the disadvantages. So radical were Howard's ideas that he advocated the complete replacement of town and country with a network of garden cities which would combine the best of both. Idealistic? Definitely, but Howard was not a man to be put off.

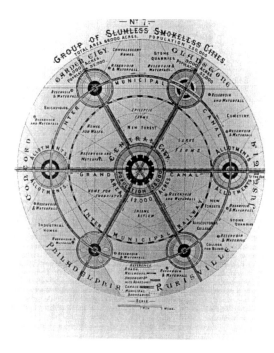

In Howard's plans, as the original garden city's population expanded, smaller satellite cities would develop around the periphery. Howard's vision included a linkage of these circles of cities across the country until all the old cities died away, leaving a brave new world of healthy and self-sufficient living.

In 1898, he published his plan for garden cities. Originally titled, *Tomorrow, A Peaceful Path to Real Reform,* it was later re-named, *Garden Cities of Tomorrow* and is still available under that title today. The book contains remarkably detailed proposals for the building, financing and running of the garden city. As Osborn points out in his 1945 preface, Howard's proposals were practical rather than scientific, yet proved so accurate that his book holds an unique place in town planning literature.

Yet, reading Howard's plan, his vision, bursting with socialist ideals, appears improbably idealistic with hindsight. To us, looking back from the twenty-first century, Howard's garden cities seem as far away as the utopias of medieval folk-lore.

'I will undertake then to show how in 'Town-country' equal, nay better, opportunities of social intercourse may be enjoyed than are enjoyed in any crowded city, while yet the beauties of nature may encompass and enfold each dweller therein: how higher wages are compatible with reduced rents and rates: how abundant opportunities for employment and bright prospects of advancement may be secured for all; how capital may be attracted and wealth created; how the most admirable sanitary conditions may be ensured; how beautiful homes and gardens may be seen on every hand; how the bounds of freedom may be widened, and yet all the best results of concert and co-operation gathered in by a happy people.'
(Howard 1946, 1965 edn. Pp48-49).

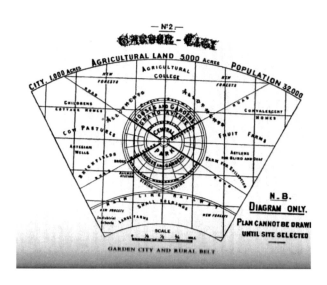

Howard's original garden city design. Note the similarity to new town designs: the central urban area containing services and shops, surrounded by homes and gardens with the agricultural green belt as the outer area.

One wonders what he would have made of contemporary Skelmersdale. The later definition adopted by the Garden Cities and Town Planning Association in 1919 is a little more pragmatic.

'A garden city is a town designed for healthy living and industry; of a size that makes possible a full measure of social life but not larger; surrounded by a rural belt; the whole of the land being in public ownership or held in trust for the community.'
(quoted in Osborn & Whittick, (1969:36).

It is important to note the emphasis on communal ownership in Howard's proposals for garden cities – a purely socialist conception. The Garden Cities and Town Planning Association definition is a little more ambiguous. The phrases 'public ownership' and 'held in trust for the community' suggest the presence of an informed state, a body managing the city on behalf of its inhabitants. We will see how Howard's original ideas had to be modified even from the start in order to gain concrete expression and how the garden city ideal was transformed into the new town concept as it was filtered through the planning policies of successive governments.

Some dismissed Howard as a crank. George Bernard Shaw referred to him as 'Ebenezer, the garden city geyser' (Sunday Times, 27.7.03). Fortunately, Howard was taken seriously by many enthusiastic socialists and philanthropists of the day. His ideas offered a possible solution to the pressing housing problems of the period and in 1899 with the help of his many supporters, who included George Cadbury, the philanthropist chocolate manufacturer, and other prominent businessmen, he formed the Garden City Association and set about planning how to put his ideas into practice.

In 1903 a company was registered and land bought for the site of the first garden city in Hertfordshire. However, the large sums required for the venture meant that in order to attract sufficient investment from hard-headed businessmen and capitalists, Howard had to compromise some of his socialist ideals. In his original plan, the whole of the garden city's income, generated through rents, was to be returned to the residents for future management of the town. The need to attract outside investment resulted in this policy being partially sacrificed in order to satisfy investors' demands for the payment of dividends. Similarly, the communal ownership of the town had to be sacrificed in order to obtain private investment. Despite these setbacks, work proceeded and for the first time, the utopian town rose from paper plans and dreams were converted to reality in the building of Letchworth Garden City. Letchworth represents a milestone as a project embracing an holistic approach to town planning – a town with central shopping areas, and separately zoned industrial and residential areas (Ward, 1994).

The choice of site is significant in the context of the history of new town planning as the garden city would be within reach of a major conurbation and would draw its population from the overcrowded city of London.

The town was designed with the help of arts and crafts architects Raymond Unwin and Barry Parker for a planned population of 32,000. The homes they built continued the philanthropic village tradition of quality and excellent design. A limited company, First Garden City Ltd., was formed to hold the assets of the town but everyone living there was a shareholder. Money received in rents was held by the company and used to finance further development.

The opening of Letchworth created huge interest around the world, particularly among socialists, and attracted crowds of visitors who would arrive via the new railway. The problems of attracting capital and industrial investment meant that the development of an economic base for the town was slow and despite the attractions of well-equipped industrial sites there were insufficient large manufacturing industries to attract the working class population that would have made significant impact on decongestion of inner city London. Two major manufacturers were Spirella Corsets and The British Tabulating Machine Company. The town attracted a number of engineering and printing firms, including J.M.Dent, the 'Garden City Press,' which mostly employed a highly skilled workforce.

Because of the difficulties of attracting manufacturing investment and due to the socialist principles on which it was organised, Letchworth, instead of providing homes for overcrowded slum-dwellers, became instead the habitat of eccentrics with alternative views; vegetarians, good-lifers etc, whom some described as cranks so that the town soon acquired a somewhat bohemian reputation (Sunday Times, 27.7.03). Developing the industrial base of the town took many years and further problems began to arise after the second world war with the nationalisation of utilities and the structure of local councils becoming more highly differentiated. Instead of control being divided amongst individual shareholders, some shareholders were able to acquire large holdings and thus controlling interests in the town's future. Eventually First Garden City Ltd. was wound up and a public corporation was formed in 1963. However, initially, the first garden city experiment was a resounding success and Howard quickly followed it up by building Welwyn Garden City.

Welwyn was also built in Hertfordshire as an overspill town for London. It featured a spinal parkway and a central shopping area which at first took the form of a single department-style store. The original holding company Welwyn Garden City Ltd passed its assets to Welwyn City Development Corporation in 1948 when the town officially became a new town. In accordance with new towns policy, the Development Corporation was wound up in due course and assets passed to the Commission for New Towns. Control finally passed to the local authority between 1978 and 1983.

These two towns formed the concrete expression of Howard's ideals. His ideas were copied worldwide but the upheaval of the first world war put an end to his experiments.

While Howard's plan was to replace big cities with smaller self-sufficient garden cities, government thoughts on town planning were primarily concerned with solving city housing problems and focused more on the solution of extending existing towns and cities rather than replacing them. From 1900 garden suburbs or garden villages began to appear on the periphery of major cities. Examples include Old Oak in Acton on the outskirts of London, Totterton Fields at Tooting and Hampstead Garden Suburb. Similar developments took place in other parts of the country, in Manchester, Liverpool, Leicester and Coventry (Ward, ibid).

These developments, however, barely touched the pressing problems of overcrowding and decay in the inner cities. Quite apart from the unsuitability of much of the housing available, the poor condition of recruits for the Boer War raised awareness of the plight of the poorer sections of the working class On the other hand the growing threat of social unrest and political action as the working classes became increasingly unionised and politically aware created insecurity amongst the better off about the retention of their position in life. The advanced system of social provision in Germany at the time was thought to be the basis of their economic strength. A home with a garden – a symbol of private space, was seen as the means of providing social stability by encouraging family interests (Ward, 1994).

An increased emphasis on town planning by those concerned about the state of the cities, led to the Garden City Association becoming the Garden City and Town Planning Association in 1908, recognising the need for radical reconstruction rather than piecemeal efforts. Crowded city centres contained decaying factories and insanitary living quarters, cheek by jowl, and entire areas of these centres were outmoded as new forms of transport developed. Redevelopment was urgently needed and it had to be controlled rather than random. At this period, however, there was little knowledge of how town planning should be achieved and no cohesive policy or training programmes for planning practice.

A typical Liverpool court, probably early 20th century. Photo by kind permission of The Four Squares.

In 1909 the Housing, Town Planning etc. Act was passed. Its main function was to consolidate town planning as a function of local government rather than of private enterprise. It authorised the planning of town extensions and new suburban areas. Despite this step towards a consistent planning policy, city housing shortages worsened between 1909 and 1914, especially for the working classes. The new garden suburbs, built at roughly 12 homes per acre, could not possibly accommodate the crowded populations of inner city slums and development was slow. Only 56 schemes had been instituted by 1914. Professional training was another problem, or rather the lack of it. A department of Civic Design was set up in Liverpool in 1909 and a professional body, The Town Planning Institute was formed in 1914. Ideas on town planning had to be co-ordinated into a consistent body of knowledge. In addition to the example of German town planning policy noted earlier, British planners drew on the French Ecole des Beaux Arts style of architecture and the influence of the American 'City Beautiful' planning approach, which included generous landscaping.

The first world war caused little physical destruction to the country's cities but the toll on human life in the trenches required a loyalty from the working classes that increased their postwar bargaining power immensely (Ward, ibid). If the threat of social unrest had lurked in the picture before the war, it surely practically dominated it afterwards. Men returning from the war had learned the power of organised combat. Their families and the families of those who did not return had made immense sacrifices. They deserved and would demand something better than the unhealthy living and working conditions endured by their fathers. The lessons of the recent revolution in Russia and the fates of the nobility and property owners there were not lost on the government of the day.

The immediate post-war period saw the development of small private projects, often referred to as 'plotlands'. These were not philanthropic ventures but profit-making schemes where entrepreneurs bought up tracts of cheap land, often near coastal areas and divided them into individual plots which were then sold off for unregulated building, often to homecoming soldiers. The homes erected on these small holdings were often of a temporary nature, old army huts or railway carriages. Examples are New Anzac on Sea, later renamed Peacehaven, in Sussex, and Woodingdean on the South Downs. These makeshift communities often had unsavoury reputations, built without regulations or adequate facilities. Many of these communities still

38

exist today, having developed into small towns with standardised homes and amenities.

From 1918 onward a succession of housing Acts were passed, mainly concerned with town planning, slum clearance and, at least on paper, with the election pledge of Lloyd George, to provide homes fit for heroes to return to (Ward 1994:42). Money from central government was set aside for social housing with an emphasis on demolishing slums and reducing overcrowding in the cities.

Woodingdean today shows little trace of its 'plotlands' origins. It is now virtually a suburb of Brighton and Hove, its shacks and railway carriage homes replaced by modern housing.

Planned decentralisation was under way. The term 'new town' was first mentioned in 1918 (Ward 1994:52) and is also mentioned in Ministry of Health reports of 1920 and 1921, differentiated from garden cities, however, by their reliance on state funding and ownership rather than co-operative ventures. Satellite towns (new, largely self-sufficient communities on the peripheries of existing cities) appeared in the 1920s; examples are Wythenshawe in Manchester and rather later, Speke in Liverpool. The plans for these communities were influenced by the American 'neighbourhood unit,' designed by Clarence Perry, where a town was to be laid out in separate estates, each with its own schools, shops and other social facilities within walking distance of the homes. Another major influence was the Radburn principle, where vehicle and pedestrian traffic was kept segregated by separate roadways and footpath systems.

City planners were aware also of the need to replace the warren of inner-city decayed homes and narrow streets, which were totally unsuitable for modern motor transport. The areas to be cleared could then be profitably utilised to house developing service industries and to fulfil the growing demand for retail outlets as more consumer goods became available. Garden suburbs were a popular choice for local authority developments but these were fairly low density and could not rehouse all the city dwellers made homeless by decentralisation. Some schemes, such as Gerard Gardens in Liverpool, combined clean modern living conditions with a relatively central location, by opting for apartment blocks with landscaped areas. Although the private building industry also expanded in the postwar period, the mass production of large peripheral estates led to a gradual reduction of quality in new building in comparison to the earlier philanthropic villages and garden cities.

Myrtle Gardens, Liverpool: one of many similar apartment complexes built after World War 1. Others included Caryl Gardens, Warwick Gardens and Gerard Gardens, the garden in the name paying homage to the garden suburb idea. All were built in the inner city area, replacing tightly packed slum courts with modern convenience living and were considered state of the art design at the time of building. Note the grassed play area, planned for child safety within the complex to be clearly visible from the flats. Some blocks also had a shop built onto a corner of the complex. Photo reproduced by kind permission of The Four Squares.

By the 1930s, agriculture had declined to such an extent that large tracts of land could be bought very cheaply, while at the same time, developments in rail and road transport meant that the outskirts of major cities were within easy reach of the centre for most workers. On the other hand, suburbanisation generated further concerns. Ribbon developments along the major arterial roads threatened to allow cities to spread further and further outwards, swallowing up smaller towns and villages. Who knew where it might end, might not the major cities end up joining up into a huge continuous conurbation? And in the uncertain period of the 1930s, with the memory of one war to end all wars still lingering in the collective consciousness and the fear of another hovering in the wings, alarm bells rang about the need to conserve agricultural land which would be needed for self-sufficiency in the event of future war. American concerns with green belt settings to enforce limits on town expansion sat well with British concerns at a national level to protect the countryside from urban sprawl, and eventually resulted in the Green Belt Act of 1938.

Having to travel further and further into the city centre for work meant increased travel costs for workers, not to mention the congestion of increased traffic heading into and out of the city each day. More people in the city meant less in the country, a reduction of social contacts and a loss of community for those remaining. All these concerns pointed to the need for new ideas in town planning.

We have traced the growth of town planning from the individual efforts of philanthropic radicals, local borough councils and private developers to the development of statutory provisions, standardised practices and the institution of professional training bodies. In the 1930s we see a move to regional planning for the future and away from localised solutions to problems. This perspective is evident in the report of the South West Lancashire Joint Advisory Committee of 1930, previously mentioned in Chapter One. Rather than specifically attempting to solve the problems of Skelmersdale, the committee subsumed the town under the general plan for the whole of the South West Lancashire region. While the regional perspective may be beneficial both in terms of making best use of finances and in terms of producing co-ordinated long-term planning strategies for large areas, it means that, as in Skelmersdale's case, the problems of small areas may be underplayed due to emphasis on the overall plan.

As well as the developing threat of war in Europe, 1930s Britain was dogged by economic depression and unemployment. These problems were compounded by the concentration of heavy manufacturing industry and coalmining in specific areas and their subsequent decline. In an area where the majority of its workforce was employed in a single industry, the failure of that industry meant massive unemployment and hardship for the whole region. One benefit of the development of regional and national planning was the recognition of this difficulty and the ability to take steps to alleviate it.

Between 1927 and 1928 the Industrial Transfer Scheme was introduced. This aimed to give subsidies to workers in areas of declining industry to encourage them to move to areas where employment was plentiful (Ward 1994). In 1934 a different approach was applied with the Special Areas Act where financial assistance was offered to enable areas of declining industry to redevelop new industrial bases, and build new model, industrial estates to encourage industries from other areas to re-locate to them. We may recall that similar inducements were offered later in the development of the new towns and such schemes were later blamed for the economic collapse that blighted Skelmersdale's growth following the honeymoon period, when its major manufacturing industries departed for greener pastures. At this point of time, however, although most of the Special Areas focused on coalmining areas, Lancashire was not designated as one of them.

We have seen then, that although town planning became increasingly co-ordinated on a national and regional level in the period between the two world wars, financial difficulties and the pressures to prepare for war placed limits on both the development of planning itself and on the end results, the concrete provision of homes, industry and transport networks. However, a gradual transformation was taking place, (with the emphasis on gradual) from a reliance on piecemeal private enterprise and local authority efforts, to increasingly state-dominated policies under direct central government control.

As the Second World War approached, awareness grew that a focused approach to planning and dealing with the ills of society was essential. The social unrest resulting in outbreaks of protest such as the Jarrow march of 1936, and the rise of right-wing groups such as Oswald Mosley's fascists, had not gone unnoticed. The need for a concerted effort to pull the nation together as war loomed may have influenced government thinking in consolidating the unco-ordinated efforts in social planning to date. This need for drastic change may have underpinned the commissioning of the enquiry into 'The Distribution of the Industrial Population,' (The Barlow Report) in 1940, a report which would have far-reaching effects on British planning policy for the future.

The Barlow Report

The Barlow Report embraced many of Ebenezer Howard's ideas on marrying town and country by decentralising major cities and dispersing their populations to underdeveloped areas.

It examined earlier projects such as garden cities and satellite towns and also evaluated trading estates such as Trafford Park in Manchester. It emphasised a requirement of local authorities to make such provisions, rather than relying on private schemes like the philanthropic villages.

The report identified a need for central government supervision to ensure effective spending and also envisaged a need for central funding to assist the development of major schemes.

Particular concern was expressed about London, its expanding size and increasing congestion, and its potential as a target for aerial attack, not just as the seat of political power but as the centre of major services and industry.

The report highlighted the way control of industry, labour and transport was currently split between several Ministries and proposed the creation of a single authority to deal with decentralisation and the redistribution of industry, to be named The National Industrial Board.

It favoured the development of garden cities or suburbs, satellite towns, trading estates and the expansion of existing small towns in suitable areas, with financial assistance for all such schemes in the early years of their development. Although it spoke of social conditions, the report's conclusions were concerned primarily with the redistribution of industry, apparently being of the opinion that social conditions would right themselves once industry was put on a secure footing.

The report was published in 1940 but by then any immediate action was forestalled by the outbreak of war in September 1939. However, the activities of war themselves had significant effects on the movement of population and industries. Ward (1994) identifies the following factors:

1, A reduction in unemployment.
2. The movement of production away from bombing targets.
3. Greater state influence and centralisation of the national economy.
Most activities

were placed under Government control, reducing the role of private enterprise.

4. A greater awareness of the value of the working classes to the economy as a whole.

5. An unprecedented mixing of the social classes, caused by the movements of war,
    brought about a greater awareness of inequality and resulted in more sympathetic
    attitudes in the middle classes and empowerment of the working classes. The need to
    create a better way of life for the working classes was seen as a reward for their
    services and loyalty.

6. The bombing of major city centres destroyed many of the old slum areas and made
    the provision of new homes unavoidably urgent.

Bomb damage in Sir Thomas Street, Liverpool, May 1941. Photo courtesy of The Four Squares.

It was clear that major redevelopment was necessary in the blitzed cities and as early as 1942 the Ministry of Works and Planning was created, beginning the momentum for re-construction even as the war progressed. A significant factor was the extent of government control over the acquisition of land and the nature of re-construction, although these controls were hotly disputed by the private sector.

Planning was transferred to the Ministry of Town and Country Planning in 1943. The Town and Country Planning (Interim Development) Act of the same year put planning under state control while the Town and Country Planning Act (1944) gave compulsory purchase powers to allow the re-construction of blitzed areas.

Plans for major reconstructions in London, Coventry and other major cities began to appear from 1941 onwards. The Dudley Report (Design For Dwellings) 1944, advocated better housing standards than in pre-war social housing. It recommended mixed developments of houses and flats with green space, organized around the neighbourhood unit, as previously described (Ward, 1994).

The Greater London Plan of 1944 focused on decentralisation and proposed an inner core surrounded by a suburban ring, the whole to be encircled by a green belt. It included radical proposals for eight completely new towns to accommodate the decentralisation of the inner London population, together with industrial and community facilities.

The Distribution of Industry Act (1945) extended the powers of the Special Areas to allow financial assistance to be given to firms in the new Special Development Areas. Merseyside was now included as a Special Development Area.

In 1945, at the end of the war, a new Labour government came to power with commitments to state ownership, a welfare state, and controlled planning. It also promised to provide every family with a good standard of accommodation (Tait,1979), but the immediate push for re-construction was hampered by postwar shortages of building materials.

The new government was interested in the concept of 'The New Town' rather than advocating existing town redevelopments. The new town was seen as the embodiment of a new postwar society, sweeping away the old and rotten, providing the good things of life – an icon to be invested with the hopes of calming postwar social unrest (Tait ibid). The Reith Committee was commissioned to prepare a series of reports on planning and the development of new towns. At this point

in time, the basis was laid for the model of the new town which would
be followed for many years and would determine the destiny of
Skelmersdale as well as that of many other small communities which
received the designation of new town status.

The First New Towns

The new town model was for a planned community of 30-50,000
population. It would be controlled by a Development Corporation,
basically under State control. The Development Corporation would
own the land involved which it would acquire under compulsory
purchase powers. The new town would be self-contained with US
style neighbourhood units and a balanced mix of social classes.

Action swiftly followed the construction of the model in the form
of the New Towns Act of 1946. The first new town designation at
Stevenage was promptly followed by Crawley, Hemel Hempstead,
Harlow, Hatford, Welwyn (its Garden City status being re-designated
to that of New Town), Basildon and Bracknell – all of which were
created to relieve pressure on London.

Other new towns were designated at New Aycliffe, Peterlee and
Patton in County Durham, East Kilbride and Glenrothes (Scotland),
Cwmbran (South Wales) and Corby (Northamptonshire). Most of
these were developed with the intention of revitalising areas of
depressed industry and social decline. This first wave of new towns
(commonly known as Mark 1 new towns) consisted of small planned
communities built on garden city lines but the original ideal of
communal ownership was omitted in favour of state control. It took
some years for the first building programme to get under way, many
of the designated towns were not built until the 1950s but as Ward
(1994) points out, they reflect the concrete statement of the post war
idea of a new model society.

THE TOWN OF THE FUTURE

■ There can be no doubt that our future towns will be as different from those we knew before the war as a radiogram is different from our first crystal set. And just as our admiration for the elegance and the greater efficiency of the modern does not in any way impair our affection for the old-fashioned, so we need have no regrets when we come to live in the town of the future.

Towns and cities damaged by the war are already considering their rebuilding plans. Residential districts, we are told, will be designed on the garden city principle of villas or semi-detached houses each with its own garden; or ten-storey blocks of flats surrounded by communal lawns, flower walks and rose arbours. It is gratifying to note that experts are planning for a ' green and pleasant land ' with plenty of space, light and fresh air. In the past, towns and cities have straggled and sprawled, capturing parts of the countryside with the same inevitable disappointment as the caging of a wild bird. The town of the future will be erect and compact, with the trees, the grass and the flowers of the country-side brought to its front doors. Schools and playgrounds for the children will be included as an integral part of the communal plan. These will be so positioned that children will not have to cross main roads on their way to school. The Shopping Centre, in view of its supreme importance to housewives, will receive very special attention. Architects, remembering the British climate, will develop the arcade principle for greater all-the-year-round convenience, specially appreciated on wet shopping days.

Ancient buildings will be restored and records and relics of a glorious past preserved. The town of the future will retain its cherished character, its unique individuality and its historical associations, yet it will sparkle and shine in its new pride.

New buildings, new services, new homes, rising up from the ruins of the old, will make for happier family life in Britain after the war. The better environment will invite us to make the most of our longer leisure and will encourage us to seek new interests within the pleasant, comfortable and healthy precincts of our new homes.

Pears

RENOWNED AS THE LEADING TOILET SOAP SINCE 1789

A Pears poster from the 1940s, reproduced here by kind permission of Unilever plc.

This slowness in developing the new town programme (only 10% of new homes built before 1955 were in new towns (Tait,1979), and a change to a Conservative government, resulted in no further new town designations in the 1950s, except for that of Cumbernauld (Scotland) in 1955, but development of the existing new towns continued and the Commission for New Towns was created in 1959 to deal with transferring the assets of the completed towns from their Development Corporations.

The new towns were seen as planning innovations, forward-looking environments for the aspiring working classes. The matching of tenants' skills to employers' requirements, while it is reminiscent of the paternalism of the earlier philanthropists, perhaps made for a harmonious work environment. The towns themselves, well designed and planned for modern transport and production and boasting excellent shopping facilities, represented a vision of modern life.

A modern view of Stevenage town centre. Stevenage was the first new town, designated in 1946 although it had been a town since medieval times. Its first estates were occupied in 1951. It had the first purpose-built traffic-free town centre in the country which was opened by the Queen in 1959.

Design from the mid 50s on was based on the Radburn principle of residential layout and made provision for car ownership. The apparent success of the first batch of new towns set the scene for a second wave in the 1960s. These were much larger planned communities, designed to accommodate the latest industries and developments in road traffic. Skelmersdale was to be the first designation.

Summary
A mixture of factors was evident in the decision to choose new towns as a planning strategy to deal with the decentralisation of major conurbations rather than satellite towns or garden suburbs. Such factors included: savings on the purchase of land and the protection of available resources; economies of the wholesale provision of public services involved in the building of a new town rather than piecemeal improvements of existing areas; the avoidance of incidental problems arising during developments by comprehensive planning and the spreading of costs over time, made possible by long term land management (Town & Country Planning Act, 1972).

The new town vision incorporated aspects of earlier utopias; green space, gardens, well designed homes and surroundings, but the execution of that vision was, however, influenced and changed by economic and political factors, the concerns of the period and the attitudes of contemporary government.

The first new towns were self-sufficient communities of relatively small populations, built either to accommodate city overspill populations or to stimulate depressed areas. They were designed for contemporary living, with good social facilities and clean, healthy environments, featuring up-to-date home design and plenty of green space. Their tenants were selected to match industrial requirements and to create a balanced social mix. The towns were overseen by centrally funded Development Corporations and their assets were transferred to the Commission For New Towns on completion.

In Chapter One we saw how the history of Skelmersdale left the town with severe problems in the period leading up to and including the Second World War. In this chapter we have seen how national and regional policies developed from older historical models of planned communities to culminate in the post-war commitment to the creation of new towns. How this model translated into the designation and development of Skelmersdale New Town will be the subject of the next chapter.

50

Chapter Three
Interpreting the postwar dream: the designation of Skelmersdale
New Town.

In this chapter we return to the history of Skelmersdale to chart life between the end of World War 2 and the early development of the new town. Drawing on insights gained in the previous chapters regarding the growth of Skelmersdale from village to mining town in the nineteenth century and the shaping of national and regional town, I will examine specific factors that led to Skelmersdale being included in the second wave of new towns designated in the 1960s. The chapter will explore the first steps to the proposed reinvention of the town from declining semi-rural community to state-of-the-art civic modernity.

When we talk about 'Skem' we tend to divide it into distinct pre- and post-new town identities. However, a quick delve into its history shows that Skelmersdale, in essence, has been a new town twice, and that what we assume to be its traditional identity was, in fact, thrust upon it in the nineteenth century in a flurry of economic and social development not dissimilar to the designation of the new town in the twentieth century.

In 1801 Skelmersdale was a tiny rural community with a population of 414. A hundred years later it had swelled to over 6000 (Sands, 1970). We have seen how the extension of Lancashire coal mining into Skelmersdale and the advent of the railway accounted for this explosion and Chapter One details how cheap, unregulated housing was rapidly erected by private landlords to accommodate the expanding population.

With the decline of mining between the 1890s and 1930s the town grew increasingly depressed, with few means of regeneration. Many of the homes in the town, originally of substandard construction, deteriorated and were subject to only piecemeal repairs. In addition, the legacy of the mines left a blighted landscape of barely disguised spoil heaps which detracted from the town's rural identity.

Arley pit spoil heap, photo reproduced by kind permission of Harold Swift.

For an area reliant on a single major source of employment, the loss of that source with the decline of the mines created major difficulties. The gradual failure of large-scale northern industries and the increasing concentration of jobs in the south of England meant that Skelmersdale shared the fate of much of the region in its inability to create employment opportunities for its residents. Job creation during this period was small scale, involving independent minor manufacturing such as the rope works or food processing establishments such as the egg-packing plant and even these offered mostly only part-time work for women.

The problem was not specific to Skelmersdale. It was part of a national epidemic, but the north of England was particularly badly affected. Formerly the heart of British mining, engineering and other major industries, the whole region was now in decline and decay in the face of foreign competition and the growth of service industries in the south.   However, as we saw in Chapter One, the problems of Skelmersdale were glossed over in regional planning reports, the implied consensus being that Skelmersdale should be left to die back to its former rural village status or be subsumed into one of its larger neighbouring communities.

This rural view of Skelmersdale provides a sharp contrast to the spoil heap shown on the previous page. Note Ashurst Beacon on the far horizon. Photo by kind permission of William Waterworth.

It is perhaps Skelmersdale's location in something of a rural idyll that ameliorated the worst effects of unemployment and decline and helped it escape the grim bleakness of other small mining and mill towns. In Chapter One, we saw how residents fondly recalled a strong community life in which they had a firm sense of place and how they took pride in their homes and their families. Such perspectives contrast sharply with the local authority concerns which continued to appear in the local press. Questions were raised in Parliament regarding the plight of Skelmersdale following the closure of White Moss Colliery in 1939 (Ormskirk Advertiser 9.2.39). Little was done in the 1930s to help the town but in the spirit of optimism and recognition of the need for future regeneration that followed the end of the Second World War, Skelmersdale was designated as a development area in 1946.

The acquisition of Development Area status meant that the town qualified as a high-priority area for the re-location of industry from other areas. Re-location of both industry and populations away from inner cities was, as we have seen, a major pre-occupation of postwar governments, but although in 1946, a list of town development schemes was announced, Skelmersdale was not one of those chosen. Regeneration in Liverpool focused on the development of garden suburbs and peripheral self-contained estates such as Speke, rather than a wholesale exodus to new towns in the surrounding countryside like the towns designated to ring London. Yet the idea must have been floating in the background of local and national consciousness. In 1946, Harold Wilson, then member of Parliament for Ormskirk, on a visit to Skelmersdale and District Horticultural Society recalled an earlier MP, Councillor Stephen King-Hall having a vision of Skelmersdale as a grand city of the future and commented that while the unemployment problem was the first thing to be tackled, once that was solved, 'then we should be able to turn our energies into making Skelmersdale as beautiful as the inhabitants of it deserve, and that is saying a lot' (Ormskirk Advertiser 15.8.46).

Employees from the straw rope works. Operations ceased in 1950 when the building was destroyed by fire. Photograph reproduced by kind permission of Harold Swift.

At times Skelmersdale had been slated, notably in the Victoria History of Lancashire, as 'a particularly bare, unpleasing district, for the most part occupied by collieries with huge banks of black refuse at intervals amongst treeless fields' (Page, 1907:282). After World War 2, hopes ran high that although some of this decay remained, Skelmersdale's fortunes were about to change for the better. Rumours that a large enterprise was about to re-locate to the area were reported in the local paper (Ormskirk Advertiser 10.10.46), and the district council announced a major new housing programme to extend until 1948. The council had been inundated with 380 applications for the tenancies of 12 new homes built on School Lane (Ormskirk Advertiser 31.10.46). Plans were revealed for 226 homes to be built on Windrows in the Ormskirk Advertiser of 7.11.46.

In November 1946, a homes, housing and planning exhibition was held at the Mission hall in Liverpool Road. The chairman of the executive committee said that Merseyside planners wanted to wipe Skelmersdale off the map but that they were going to build a new Skelmersdale. Alderman King said that Skelmersdale represented a relic of the bad days of the industrial revolution but now a new start had been made to provide for the needs of the people (Ormskirk Advertiser 28.11.46).

Throughout the immediate postwar period and the 1950s, improvements continued. Many of the slag heaps were covered and landscaped. An account of the provision of gas supplies in the area to 1949 contradicts the glum picture of Skelmersdale portrayed in the Victoria History:

Modern view of the river Tawd in Skelmersdale. Photo courtesy of David Baker

'In the present writer's view this is either an unduly harsh judgement or the Skelmersdale landscape has improved during the last half-century. Coal mining has long since ceased there, slag heaps and disused colliery railroads are now grass grown and pithead gear and buildings have disappeared. The area certainly is not qualified for inclusion in any book concerned with the charm of the English countryside but it presents gently undulating rural vistas, fringed by numerous stretches of woodland and dotted with sturdy stone cottages and an occasional farmstead. The small river Tawd flows through the township on its way to the shady woods and pleasant meadows of Lathom' (Harris, 1956:227).

The new homes at Manor Farm were completed and the Co-operative Wholesale Society became a major employer. Brocks Fireworks employed 150 more but still these changes were minor in the face of the town's unemployment and housing problems. The decline in the population meant depleted revenue for the district council which prevented it from regeneration on a scale necessary to create a major impact.

A perusal of the newspapers of the period reveals a persistent rumour that Skelmersdale was under consideration as the site for a

new town, yet there is little concrete discussion of the matter, nor any
direct information. It is hard to tell whether there was a real lack of
knowledge about the possibility of new town designation, whether the
prospect was considered to be just a castle in the air, not worthy of
serious consideration, or whether caution was exercised by all
concerned in the face of uncertainty. On the surface and with
hindsight, in view of comments to come after the designation, it
appears that the local authority was not fully informed by central
government as to its plans for Skelmersdale and that the regional
authority held a somewhat ambivalent position between the two.

In the early 1950s, few Skelmersdale people had ties with
Liverpool. In 1951 Lancashire County Council suggested Leyland,
Garstang or Parbold as a possible new town site but strong opposition
from local residents of these communities led to Skelmersdale being
considered instead, with the support of Skelmersdale Urban District
Council (Tait,1979). At the same time, the government was
considering similar developments at Kirkby, Bootle and Widnes.

Despite these considerations, the passenger rail link to
Skelmersdale was closed in 1956, although goods traffic continued
until 1963 (Sands, 1970). This closure put pressure on bus services
and the existing road system which included many unadopted roads in
unsatisfactory states of repair (Ormskirk Advertiser, 21.2.57).

Beaman's entry c.1960. Photo courtesy of Harold Swift.
The town contained many houses in need of urgent renovation or
demolition and council houses were hard to come by. Thomas Yates
(undated 1970s?) recounts the difficulties of getting a pensioner's

bungalow in 1960. Norman Lyon in an interview with the author, recalled that many homes in old Skelmersdale were in a poor state and that some roads were little more than dirt tracks.

In the face of these concerns and the desperate employment situation, it is easy to understand why the Urban District Council gave support to proposals for extensive new development. An initial proposal for a new town was considered inappropriate and the matter was then reconsidered as a town development scheme which would have meant that control would remain in the hands of the local authority. Discussion about this went on for several years, during which the district council claimed that they were kept in the dark about the proposals and the discussion.

This indecision created a difficult situation. The town was in dire need of homes and jobs but new industries would not invest while the future of the town was so uncertain. Major new building and planning was virtually suspended while everyone waited for the Ministry to make up its mind as to Skelmersdale's fate. The council found itself in the undesirable position of having to turn away private house building proposals because if Skelmersdale was designated as a new town, the land and planning permission would come under the control of a development corporation.

Although complaints about this were voiced sporadically in the press, the general population seemed to be unaware of the impending changes that might be forced upon them. There is little information in the newspapers and virtually nothing in response from the public until just before the designation. At that time, the majority of working people in the town were employed outside in Wigan, Ormskirk or St Helens. Norman Lyon, a young teacher at the turn of the decade, travelled daily to Wigan; the focus of his life was on his work and the negotiations had little impact on his daily existence.

In the interim, small scale schemes continued to be implemented, including tree planting and landscaping at Kiln Lane and small council housing projects of less than 50 homes.

In May 1957 an UDC meeting proclaimed that Skelmersdale was undergoing a revolution, and argued that continuing improvements were helping to overcome the image of the town as a place in decline. The possibility of Skelmersdale becoming an overspill site for 50,000 Merseyfolk was touched on but not debated as being, "out of council hands" (Ormskirk Advertiser 30.5.57).

At this point, although the decision to create an overspill development in the area had been decided at governmental and regional level, the choice of site was still in question. Skelmersdale UDC was not fully involved in the discussions on the town's future until July 1957 when they were invited to meet with Lancashire County Council officers and were then officially informed that a total overspill population of 160,000 was proposed to be shared between Skelmersdale and Kirkby. By September 1957, the Ormskirk Advertiser was describing Skelmersdale of the future as "a modern show place of a town" (12.9.57). Following further discussions with LCC and the Ministry, Skelmersdale UDC finally approved the proposed development plan in October 1957.

The councillors emphasised the need to consider humanitarian grounds; the Mersey people who would come should be welcomed and it was the duty of more fortunate people to assist them to enjoy fresh air and clean homes. Another justification put forward was that the new development would safeguard the continuation of Skelmersdale as an independent entity. Because of its location and size, it was in danger of declining into a village to be subsumed under the auspices of Ormskirk or Wigan, if the new town status was not accepted. Finally, the council felt that the existing population could only benefit from the new homes and employment prospects that the development would bring. Even so, at this late stage, although it was definite that Skelmersdale would undergo major regeneration, it still had not been decided whether it would be in the form of a town development scheme under local authority control, or whether it would be a new town with a centrally controlled development corporation.

From then on, reports began to appear in the press, suggesting that local bodies, including the parish church, were making plans to accommodate the proposed influx. These were small news items with little sense of urgency. There was virtually no reaction from local residents in correspondence to the newspaper. The local authority plodded on with its original development plans. In 1958 the long awaited secondary school finally opened and at the opening ceremony, Councillor Farrimond spoke of "a new Jerusalem in England's green and pleasant land," to be built by the young with, "a flame of freedom in their souls" (Ormskirk Advertiser 19.6.58).

Pupils at Skelmersdale Secondary Modern School, 1958. Photo supplied by Val Keenan.

It was not until the week before Christmas (when naturally most people were preoccupied with the forthcoming celebrations) that the proposed development made the front page of the Advertiser, but even then it was not the main story. A public meeting was to be held at the town hall on the 26th January 1959 to discuss the plans with local people.

By the time the new year broke, people seemed to be getting the message that some sort of development would be taking place in the town. There were mixed responses, some supporting the humanitarian treatment of the newcomers, others resisting the proposals at any costs. Still no definitive statement was forthcoming from central government as to what form the new development would take. Most were under the impression that the changes would be gradual, over a period of many years, and would thus cause minimal disruption to the life of the town.

Rumours ran through the community. The plan might not materialise for years, if at all; or work might begin within two years. The Advertiser commented on 1st January that the planned meeting would, "pierce the fog that has surrounded the whole issue," but in another article revealed that negotiations had reached, "a very advanced stage indeed."

The town hall meeting was packed as the people of Skelmersdale began to wake up to the implications of the new town proposals and questions were asked about the role of the indigenous population – would they be passed over in favour of the new residents where jobs and housing were concerned? Many were under the impression that the nature of the town would be unchanged; that Sandy Lane would continue to form the town centre, with the new development gradually spreading outwards from the traditional core.

The Ormskirk Advertiser reported that building would proceed from the town hall out at a rate of 350 homes per year, "a slow even progress so that everything grows up together with a minimum of discomfort and upheaval," (12.4.59). Anyone who has seen the film footage of the huge building site which Skelmersdale became in the early 1960s can only sympathise with such naivety and the disillusionment which must have followed.

By August of 1959 the focus of public concern seemed to shift from the preservation of the old town to the creation of a bright new one. Although many people still felt that the new development might never take place, there seemed to be an acceptance that the plans would go ahead regardless of the townspeople's wishes. At a talk given by the author at Skelmersdale library, original Skelmersdale residents told how they felt that council dignitaries had made their minds up to accept the new town and refused to listen to the voices of local people. Instead of fighting the plans, importance was laid on the preservation of areas of natural beauty and attention to good design and quality structures; on the need to make a good job of this new venture.

By 1960 the plans were commonly referred to as being for a new town, although still no concrete decision had been made. Large industries, including Pilkingtons and Callow Engineering were already looking at Skelmersdale as a possible location for new enterprise.

In September 1960, the news broke that the Skelmersdale development would be built under the New Towns Act, controlled by a development corporation and that the work would commence within five years. This set off a furore of debate. A letter to the Editor at the Ormskirk Advertiser asked, "Will the new town be just a dormitory?" The headline read, "Danger of a place without a soul," (22.9.60). In the same issue, Councillor Davies referred to the decision as, "this bombshell that the minister has dropped."

On another page the headline shouted, "A Town Torn In Two: Shock Plan Splits Skem," as residents took up positions for and against the influx of Merseysiders and the proposed redevelopment. For some the prospect of dumping an uprooted urban population on their doorstep was "ghastly" (Guardian, 17.9.60:12). Others feared the destruction of the town's character. These were arguments that had been aired many times in the previous years but the sudden vehemence with which they were now mooted, suggests that only now was the indigenous population becoming truly aware of the momentous changes that were coming; that until this time they had languished under the comforting misconception that the whole scheme was just another government pipedream.

In November 1960 a party of Skelmersdale councillors visited the new towns of Welwyn Garden City and Hatfield and returned with glowing reports of social life in these communities. The following March, arguments and indecision were finally ended when central government made a draft order of designation for a new town at Skelmersdale, initially comprising homes for 50,000 people with the provision for a further 30,000 to be achieved by natural growth.

The justification for choosing new town status rather than town development was that the area chosen would include four different local authorities which would create difficulties in co-ordinating control of the work. Furthermore, local authority budgets would struggle to provide the necessary services for a large incoming population, so a single governing body with central government funding was deemed more appropriate.

The necessary consultation process received only sixteen objections, despite the fact that over fifty farmers would lose their livelihoods as a result of the new building. Most people seemed to feel that there was no point in objecting and that they should just accept the inevitable (Ormskirk Advertiser 12.10.61). Council members welcomed the order, perhaps relieved that a decision had finally been reached. Councillor Farrimond remarked that there was no reason why Skelmersdale should not be the finest new town of all and the vicar of Skelmersdale described the present town as a dying town of old property and said that the new town was a fine solution and the influx of new people would add to its culture (Ormskirk Advertiser, ibid).

At the subsequent public enquiry in June, few objections were raised; mostly from other local councils concerned at the impact the adjacent new town would have on their districts, farmers concerned with the loss of their livelihoods and residents concerned about possible loss of visual amenities. These were largely overruled by the Minister although government officials did visit local farms and beauty spots as part of their considerations.

The UDC council meeting took place as usual in July 1961 but major chain stores were already making plans for branches in the new town, well before the results of the public enquiry were revealed. On 9th October 1961, Skelmersdale was officially designated as a new town.

What protest there had been ceased as the townspeople got to grips with their new status. They had little inkling of what lay in store as they pictured a gentle and gradual redevelopment and were unprepared for the radical destruction and reconstruction that would soon follow.

On 14th December 1961, the officers of the Skelmersdale Development Corporation were appointed and their offices set up in Liverpool. Three of the appointees were from Liverpool, one from Manchester and only one from Skelmersdale UDC. The lives of people in Skelmersdale were about to be changed in ways they never imagined and their town would rise anew, in the eyes of some a replica of Blake's New Jerusalem, in the eyes of others a new Babylon.

Farmland which would soon become the site of the Concourse shopping centre. Photo by kind permission of William Waterworth.

Chapter Four

First Steps

We have already examined the postwar enthusiasm for building, not just new homes but a new society. Mumford (1945) in an addendum to Howard (1946), writes of the old inadequate areas of inner cities in the face of rapid technological change, including the advent of the motor car and the explosion of movement it created, but he also points to changes in societal thinking. Mumford argues that a move occurred away from selfishness and laissez-faire capitalism towards a greater regard for the well-being of our fellows. While this may seem a somewhat rosy tinted viewpoint, it must be granted that such philosophical claims were given concrete form with the advent of the welfare state.

We have seen how the idealism of planned utopias influenced town planning in the first half of the 20th century and certainly the postwar dream of a new and better society is evident in the arguments for the creation of the new towns. It is also clear that change had to come as new technologies made the facilities of existing towns and cities obsolete. Yet Tait (1979) argues that the Skelmersdale Development Corporation designed Skelmersdale New Town according to rational, scientific principles. This claim is not as cold as it seems. The application of the most up to date theory in town planning and building construction shows a concern with design at its best and an enthusiasm for the principle of the new town concept that goes beyond cold rationalism.

In this chapter we will explore how these approaches combined to produce the master plan for Skelmersdale New Town and trace the first steps in putting the adopted principles into practice.

The Immediate Post-Designation Period

Two months after the designation decision of October 1961, the first
officers of Skelmersdale Development Corporation were appointed
although the Corporation itself was not formally constituted until the
25th January 1962. The board of officers included a woman, Mary
Kemshall, appointed to give the feminine focus on homes, play areas
and social facilities for housewives.
Councillor Farrimond from
Skelmersdale Council was the only
representative with local connections.
The Board was chaired by A.J.
Kentish Barnes, a peer of the realm
from Caldy in Cheshire.

*A.J. Kentish Barnes, Chairman of
Skelmersdale Development
Corporation.*

In January 1962, the post of General Manager of the Skelmersdale
Development Corporation was advertised. The Chairman of the Board
stated that it would be eighteen months before there were any visible
signs of development but did advise that the new town would be
planned as a motor car town (Ormskirk Advertiser 1.2.62). It is
significant that this feature is the one major influence to be mentioned
at this early stage. From a present day perspective, it is difficult for us
to appreciate the upheaval that the rapidly developing deployment of
motor vehicles was making to life in the 1960s. Not only did every
family aspire to have a car and every factory worker aspire to work in
one of the burgeoning car manufacturers, but the patterns of
movement created by the capacity for travel for both work and leisure,
created huge shifts in the perceptions of town planners. Inner city
roads and streets proved inadequate to cope with the ever increasing
flow of traffic.

Thus the motor car was perhaps a major factor in the adoption of the new town idea, planned to start from scratch with modern road systems, rather than attempting to fit new patterns of travel on old road systems built for the horse and cart and a slower way of life. The impact this made on people's lives may be assessed by this report written a year later in the Skelmersdale Parish magazine for December 1963:5.

'You will have heard a lot (perhaps too much) about the Buchanan Report (*Buchanan 1963)* but there is no intention of aplogising for writing about it in your parish magazine because just at this time in Skelmersdale we are having a foretaste of what is examined in the report and what must come to all who live in town in this twentieth century.'

The Chief Architect for the new town, L. Hugh Wilson, who would prepare the master plan, was not appointed until November 1962. Wilson, like many of the early SDC employees, had previously worked on the last of the Mark 1 new towns, Cumbernauld in Scotland, so he was well versed in the requirements of new town planning.

In February 1962, the Corporation advertised for a Chief Finance Officer and a Chief Engineer and by Spring, land at the top of Sandy Lane was earmarked for the headquarters of the Skelmersdale Development Corporation. (The building is now occupied by the Co-operative Bank).

In May, George G. Watson, another Cumbernauld employee, was appointed as General Manager of Skelmersdale Development Corporation and in June, David Hughes, also from Cumbernauld was appointed. The local populace must have viewed these appointments with trepidation, their lives being put in the hands of strangers who knew little of the history and culture of the area but they did have the expertise in planning and executing a design for a new town which was essential if there was to be any chance of success. Hughes actually did have local connections; he was originally from Oldham and had worked for Lancashire County Council in the 1950s.

At this stage, the SDC headquarters was planned to have a staff of 250. The cost of building the new town was estimated at £80,000,000 and the deadline for completion was 1982.

In the meantime, however, life in Skem went on much as usual. The council continued its programme of minor repairs and small housing projects and in March 1962, it authorised the building of 92 new council homes.

Small employment opportunities surfaced with the re-opening of Crow Colliery in March 1962 but by then most Skem miners were working in St Helens pits. Brock Fireworks were still taking on trainees at a starting wage of £6 a week but these were minor events compared to the rumours of large businesses planning to come to the new town. Hopes of exciting new career opportunities must have escalated.

Crow colliery shortly before the new town development began.
Photo courtesy of Harold Swift.

An article in the Lancashire Evening Post (15.3.62) proclaimed that Skelmersdale would be the town of the 1970s and called the proposals 'an exciting new venture.' It went on to state, 'by now residents are very obviously aware that within a few years huge ultra-modern estates, shopping centres and factories will rise from the surrounding green countryside they have prized so highly.' There is no mention here of slagheaps or dilapidated housing or of some of the fears that Skelmersdale people were now voicing.

In May, Labour gained control of Skelmersdale Council with an emphasis on the creation of new homes despite the prospect of thousands of houses to be built by SDC. Perhaps fears remained that the new town properties would be reserved for overspill families while the indigenous population's need for housing was pressing.

A health committee report voiced concern about the state of privately owned properties in Penny and Union Streets (now the area known as Pennylands). The landlords were threatened with demolition orders unless major repairs were affected. A public health inspector's report of July 1962 recommended demolition as 36 of the 39 homes were unfit (Ormksirk Advertiser 12.7.62).

Protests immediately came from the residents of these streets, declaring that they were proud of their homes and resentful of the published implication that they were slums. Council officials attempted to soothe ruffled feathers by pointing out that although some of the homes were 'little palaces,' their location among poorly maintained properties could not save them from a general demolition order. Also to be considered was the fact that despite being immaculately maintained, many of these homes had been built a hundred years or so ago, and could not pass modern standards with regards to sanitation and light facilities. Bringing them up to modern requirements would cost more than demolishing and rebuilding the whole area.

At the same time the Highways Committee was deploring the state of Skelmersdale roads and streets. Many still needed conversion from gas lamps to electric lighting, and some streets still consisted of unmade surfaces.

Despite these problems of deterioration, Skelmersdale seems to have been a hotspot of activity for local youth. The snack bar in Sandy Lane boasted a juke box which apparently attracted crowds of teenagers from as far away as Kirkby and Melling. (Ormskirk Advertiser 23.8.62). Complaints of noise led to an order for its removal and a revoking of the owner's licence, but this was dismissed on appeal to Ormskirk magistrates and the juke box was given permission to return.

The news for Skelmersdale was not all bad. In July the council approved plans for a 50 bed pensioners' home at the junction of Kiln Lane and Church Road to be named Beacon View and White Moss football club announced plans for covered accommodation for 200 spectators at their ground.

In October Skelmersdale Council approved plans for another 47 new homes but housing in the town was at a premium. Proposals for new private residential developments were having to be refused because of uncertainty as to the proposed sites of new town building.

Callow Engineering, the first major firm to announce its planned removal to Skelmersdale New Town from its established base in Kirkby, requested council tenancies for its key workers, while the transfer was being effected. They also requested an improved mail and telephone service but it was the housing demand that caused the biggest problem for Skelmersdale Council. These incoming keyworkers were seen as outsiders who were not entitled to council homes ahead of the extensive waiting list of existing residents. The same problem was likely to emerge on a greater scale when the staff of the Skelmersdale Development Corporation began to expand, given that most of those employed would be from outside the local area.

Skelmersdale Council found itself in a somewhat rocky position. Not only did it have to deal with negotiation with the SDC, Lancashire County Council and the voting population, but there were proposals from Liverpool to include Skelmersdale and Ormskirk in a new Merseyside Council, which would mean a completely different ballgame, a proposition that was robustly opposed by both towns. At the same time, Upholland Council continued to dither about whether to opt for inclusion in the new town administration or not. At times, Skelmersdale's councillors must have felt beleaguered; they were being put in a position where they would be subject to national scrutiny in view of the futuristic plans for the new town, yet their whole tradition and culture was of a small mining and agricultural community. One has to admire the fortitude and courage with which they approached their task.

Plans for new building in Skelmersdale left the council with some concerns about finding names for new streets. Although at times, it looks as if the council blindly carried on with their own proposals without concerning themselves about the ethereal plans for the new town, in fact the new town was never far from their thoughts. In November of 1962, a council meeting to name new streets for a new-build project, gave consideration to the fact that names with local connections would also be needed for the many new streets to be created by the new town. Around this time, a suggestion was made that Skelmersdale should have a coat of arms. This may seem fanciful but Skelmersdale had already been approached by a national tourist organization, asking for the streets to be decked with flower baskets etc, in order to enhance the experience of the many visitors that were expected to flock to the town.

A piece of crested ware made by Savoy China, bearing a Skelmersdale coat of arms. It depicts mining scenes, a colliery, a miner and female

colliery worker, a pair of clogs and miner's pick and lamp. However, Savoy China closed down in 1933 so this piece is from an earlier time in Skelmersdale's history. I have never seen this crest anywhere else so wonder if it was created especially by the firm.

By the end of 1962, although there were no concrete signs of the new town, the local populace was to some extent aware of the coming changes. Skelmersdale Council, while carrying on with their planned programme of minor building and maintenance, was considering some of the impact that the new town would have. A skeleton staff was in place at the Skelmersdale Development Corporation to oversee plans for the town. In the Christmas Eve edition of the Ormskirk Advertiser, the chairman of SDC was photographed showing plans for the new town to his colleagues. He is quoted as saying that 1500 families per year would be expected to move to the town during the peak period of construction but he emphasised that the town would be a self-contained community, not a slum clearance project or an employment relief scheme. In his opinion, people would be voluntarily attracted to the town for housing and work.

While it may be true that new towns attracted young, entrepreneurial families, keen to better themselves, we will see that quite stringent conditions were applied to those wanting to move to Skelmersdale New Town. The Development Corporation planners were at pains to ensure that the new town would not be one huge council estate and vowed that diversity would be at the heart of the town's design. Planning for a balanced age structure would be one way of achieving the desired population mix.

However, no matter how much care goes into plans on paper, the attempt to translate them into practice is invariably skewed by unforeseen conditions and human error. Just as the population of Letchworth, the first garden city, failed to attract the social mix envisaged by Ebenezer Howard and his associates, so the plans made for Skelmersdale with the best of intentions, while initially successful, were thrown off track by developments in the wider social and economic climate.

At this point, however, all seemed rosy. Concerns voiced were of a minor nature such as whether the incoming tenants would be able to afford to furnish their new properties. Social expectations would be high. No one would want to bring old outdated furniture to these brand new, state-of-the-art homes and everyone would want the latest electrical appliances that were springing into shops at an alarming rate. There were fears that tenants might get into debt, overspending on hire purchase commitments. Looking back at this from our current perspective, with the proliferation of electronic and electrical appliances that we now have, together with our acceptance of debt culture, these fears seem laughable. However, in the early 1960s, after the austerity of the immediate postwar years, the sudden explosion of scientific developments into home appliances created an almost fairytale world of desirable goodies which manufacturers, then as now, did all they could to portray as necessary for good living. In this period, also, buying on credit was a relatively new experience and the 'never-never' promised access to luxury and self-indulgence, with retailers, as always, happy to let customers run up big hire purchase bills.

So the new town planners talked of providing advice bureaux to help the new population manage the finances of living in this unfamiliar environment. This may smack of the paternalism of Victorian philanthropic villages but together with the emphasis on achieving a desirable mix of classes and ages, demonstrates concern for the emotional and financial welfare of the new residents. We see just how carefully detailed the plans were to be and how much homage they paid to the original new town ideal. Lessons had been learned during the 15 year development of the Mark 1 new towns and the planning of Skelmersdale New Town drew on these lessons with the ideal of making Skelmersdale the flagship of a new and improved programme of new towns.

Away from the planning and discussions taking place in government departments and the SDC offices, it was New Year in Skelmersdale. The winter of 1962-3 was one of the worst winters on record but it didn't prevent New Year celebrations in the town. The Mothers' Union held a trip to Liverpool and the Royal Court Theatre. The New Year social at Skem Labour Club was so full that people were turned away. In those days people still made their own entertainment. The programme at the club that night included local entertainers the Green brothers, Arthur Pennington, Eric Roughley and Walter Middlehurst.

Most of the country struggled to keep going despite banks of snow that stuck solid from December through till March. A St. Bernard dog (ironically) was found collapsed in the snow and was revived at Skelmersdale police station's fire until its owner collected it (Ormskirk Advertiser 3.1.63).

In early January Skelmersdale council awaited tenders for 37 more homes to be built on Church Farm. At this point councillors were still under the impression that the SDC had no plans for development in the old town. Some councillors were therefore upset that applications for minor improvements were having to be referred to the SDC before they could make decisions. Already a separation was visible between the corporation members, nearly all out-of-towners, experienced in new town planning but knowing little about Skelmersdale, and the local council officials. Councillor Davies probably spoke for many when he said he felt they were 'stooges in someone else's hands' (Ormskirk Advertiser 10.01.63).

The point was illustrated in February by the appointment of the Chief Legal Officer for the Development Corporation, Edgar Bradbury, who came from Deal in Kent to take up the post. He was originally from St. Helens so perhaps at least had some knowledge of the local area and its people.

Meetings of Skelmersdale council committees demonstrated growing concern in February and March of 1963. While still trying to decide how to deal with Callow Engineering's repeated requests for keyworker housing, the council also had to decide the fate of houses in Sherratt Street and were unable to get any decision from the development corporation until their master plan for the new town was completed. Relations were further soured later in the year, when SDC opposed an application to build a new Comrades club on Witham Road, after council officials had already approved the plan.

Despite these difficulties the council was able to go ahead with demolition orders on the old cotton mill in Taylor Street and on houses in Peel Street and Summer Street. A sad day came with the granting of a demolition order on the seventeenth century Sephton Hall in Tawd Road.

Sephton Hall, also known as Bullens Farm.One of many 17th century farmhouses demolished to make way for the new town. Picture reproduced by kind permission of Harold Swift.

The current owner had applied to build houses on the cleared site. A suggestion was made to save the hall by turning it into a folk museum of old Skelmersdale. How nice that would have been, but despite this and other objections, the order was granted.

It almost sounds as if Skelmersdale was being dismantled bit by bit but at this time the changes must have appeared minor and piecemeal. On the plus side, Beaconsfield Footwear was becoming an increasingly important employer, achieving production of up to 7000 pairs of shoes a week. This, at least, was something for the original population to be proud of as Beaconsfield was (and still is) a family firm belonging to the Houlgraves, which had operated in Skelmersdale for many years, before the new town had ever been thought of, and remains (as Hotter Shoes) one of the most successful and enduring firms in Skelmersdale to this day.

Another successful firm at the time was Brock's fireworks, one of only three factories in the UK, it made fireworks and pistol caps which were popular with junior cowboys at the time when Western films were flooding in from America. The factory was on the former site of White Moss colliery at Slack Brow, off Wigan Road, not far from the Fox and Goose Inn. The factory was in production for many years, employing up to 200 workers which may seem a small figure in comparison with industries planned for the new town, but when we consider the low population before the new town influx, the firm must have been a significant employer.

For the locals, life went on much as usual with regular club meetings and outings. However in March, the landlord of the Knowl Brow pub made headlines in the local press when he declared that Skem people were churlish and had made him feel unwelcome since coming to take up his tenancy from Warrington. He went on to say he felt alone and friendless and hoped that the new town would bring changes. (Ormskirk Advertiser (7.3.63). It's hard to justify this in comparison with the praise given to Skelmersdale people for welcoming evacuees in WW2, so one has to wonder if personal differences played a part in the situation.

In April, Skelmersdale hosted the Liverpool Premier Cycle Racing Club's two day event which consisted of a 60 mile road race, an 18 mile time trial and a further 42 mile road race, and this before Skelmersdale's superb new road system was laid for the new town. Also in April, Callow Engineering secured a £9000 order from Holland. At the time this would be a major achievement and it gave extra weight to Callow's continued demand for housing for its key and service workers.

As life went on in Skelmersdale, SDC was working behind the scenes, occasional pronouncements reminding the population that the inevitable was under way. Assurances were given that farmland would be kept in production until needed and that 'adequate compensation' would be given (Ormskirk Advertiser 24.2.63).How this translated in relation to farmers' expectations will be seen later. Negotiations were under way for West Lancashire Water Board to supply water to the new town and SDC announced that no aerials or overhead cables would be allowed in the new developments. A footpath system was planned, intended to keep pedestrians and children safe from traffic and landscaping to residential areas was scheduled to take place before people moved in. In reality, it would be several years before the landscaping grew up to form the pleasing picture presented. By June the SDC headquarters on the High Street was almost completed and in July, the first staff moved in. Things were moving quickly now; site servicing for two areas of housing was due to commence in October. 5-6000 homes were to be built at New Church Farm with an accompanying industrial area off Wigan Road by the Fox and Goose Inn, (the Gillibrands estate).

At this stage, perhaps, plans for the new town developments impacted more on the wider community than the indigenous population. Plans for a new district general hospital at Ormskirk were approved in March 1963 with the agenda of the new town in mind (Ormskirk Advertiser 14.3.63.), even though a hospital at Skelmersdale was included in SDC's original plan, to be sited in the central part of the designated area, not far from where ASDA now stands. Building for the new Ormskirk hospital however, was not expected to take place before 1970.

The age-old problem of burial places in Skelmersdale raised its head again. An unsuccessful attempt to acquire land at Manor Grove resulted in the problem of dying once more being shelved in favour of the needs of the living. A cemetery is marked on the original SDC plan but as this is located off Liverpool Road, it may refer to the pre-existing cemetery at St. Richard's church. However, the cemetery at St Paul's is not marked on this map so it may be that the SDC originally had plans to acquire burial land at the rear of Liverpool Road. Much of the land there is unsuitable for burial purposes anyway; in the 1990s, test graves were dug on Liverpool Road allotments with a view to acquiring the site as a burial space but due to the deep bed of clay beneath the soil, the holes filled with water and were pronounced unsuitable, much to the relief of the plot holders.

The demand for keyworker housing both by incoming industries and SDC itself was perhaps slightly eased by the construction of 25 private homes on School Lane, named as Millbrook Close. These sold at £3500 and some were bought by SDC staff.

Despite planning for the new town being well under way, concerns were still being voiced. Liverpool councillors were reported in the local press as saying they would prefer to house Liverpool people within the city and the Campaign for the Protection of Rural England (CPRE) argued for an end to new towns in South Lancashire, voicing fears for the green belt and the countryside.

In June the townspeople received a major shock when Councillor Farrimond was found dead at his home. His body had lain for some time until it was discovered by his nephew on the 4th June (Ormskirk Advertiser 6.6.63). Cllr. Farrimond had been a major political figure in the town and a leading proponent of the new town proposals. He was the sole Skelmersdale representative invited onto the SDC board. His passing left a vacancy that would later be filled by Cllr. Margaret Green.

In July, Sir Keith Joseph, the Conservative Housing Minister visited Liverpool to inspect housing conditions and came under criticism from Liverpool councillors for the government's insistence on pursuing new town policies against the wishes of the people. The Liverpool councillors argued that the government's attitude prevented their favoured alternative of housing being built on the outskirts of Liverpool at Croxteth, Speke, Fazakerley and West Derby, due to the imposition of green belt restrictions.

This was just distant news to most of the Skelmersdale residents who felt little connection to the city of Liverpool and who were perhaps more concerned with their annual summer pursuits. The British Legion Queen was crowned on Skem Cricket Field on August Bank Holiday and there was a baby competition, morris dancing and country dancing displays. The population of the town had only grown by 93 in the previous ten years to a total of 6309 (Ormskirk Advertiser 25.7.63.) but the Ormskirk Advertiser, perhaps with a view of things to come, opened an office in Sandy lane that month and from then on, Skelmersdale began to have its own page in the paper. Even more significantly from early 1963 Skelmersdale gained its own newspaper, the Skelmersdale Reporter. Also in August, Martins Bank opened a branch in Sandy Lane and a new Motor Club began to meet at the Co-op hall. Skelmersdale Congregational Church revived its garden party which had not been held for the past sixty years. It seemed that the new town plans were breathing fresh life into the community.

Similarly, despite its detractors, the new town to be was obviously attracting the interest of businesses and investors. A discussion of industrial prospects in Skelmersdale at a meeting of the Lancashire and Merseyside Industrial Development Association heralded the new town as the hope of the future for Merseyside (Ormskirk Advertiser 1.8.63).

In September, Callow Engineering was in the news again still demanding homes for its keyworkers. The council appeared torn between its duty to prioritise homes for existing tenants and the fear of obstructing new industry and being thought backward and provincial. Callow claimed it was losing orders and Cllr. Margaret Green argued that 'many eyes are looking at Skelmersdale New Town' and that the town was the centre of a project of worldwide interest, so the local council had to look beyond local concerns (Ormskirk Advertiser 5.9.63.). Callow then submitted plans to build homes in Bromilow Road and these were approved subject to a condition that the currently unadopted road should be made into a proper road at the firm's expense.

Also in September came the news of the imminent closure of the last railway link to Skelmersdale. This had only been a goods line since passenger services had been withdrawn in 1956 but it must have felt like a death knell at the time. The decision to close the line seems so foolish with the prospect of a major town development in the immediate future, but we have to consider it in the wider context of the national policy of rail line closures that was in operation at the time. The government attempted to soften the blow by saying that the line could be reinstated if necessary but this was never going to be a viable possibility. The old railway line has become the major road into the new town from Ormskirk, aptly named Railway Road and although, over the years, residents have been vocal in their demands for an accessible railway station, nothing has been done. Every few years, suggestions have been put forward for a suitable railway line and hopes raised but so far nothing has come of them. Nevertheless, towards the end of 2013, proposals were being considered for a railway link with a station in the town centre close to the site of Skelmersdale college so once more we wait with bated breath for further developments.

In September, L. Hugh Wilson, the chief architect for the new town produced an interim report on the planning proposals. He began by saying that a paper plan should not become the idol of developers, thus indicating an awareness of the need for flexibility. One of the major emphases of this report was the regard for a high prospective level of car ownership. As well as the design of a road system suited to high levels of vehicles, the plans also included plentiful provision of parking spaces and a separation of vehicular and pedestrian traffic by means of a separate footpath system. All amenities were to be sited within easy walking distance of residential homes. This immediately ruled out Sandy Lane's chances of remaining the town centre, as it was situated on the edge of the proposed new town development. Instead, a central main shopping area would be surrounded by housing estates containing smaller shopping centres. These design features were easily predictable as they followed the very similar designs used in earlier new towns.

The report further stated that, 'The town should have a coherent structure which can easily be appreciated by those who live in and visit it," (Wilson, 1963:2). The mismatch between intentions and reality is evident in the numerous tales of getting lost amongst New Skelmersdale's roundabouts told by new residents and visitors alike to this day.

Industrial areas were to be kept separate from residential areas but should be distributed in different parts of the town to allow easy access. Consideration was also given to maintaining a strong green belt round the town.

Building was to take place in controlled stages, with each phase including the provision of the full range of required facilities. The town would cover 4029 acres with a planned final population of 80,000. Again the immediate practical result was far from these idealistic statements. Early residents recall muddy landscapes and having to shop at mobile vans for some time before shops etc. were up and running.

One purpose of the interim report was to attract industry from Merseyside as a priority but if insufficient regional business interest was created, firms from elsewhere would be accepted. Three industrial areas were planned: 150 acres at Stormy Corner (now the Stanley industrial estate), 125 acres south of Old Skelmersdale, (Gillibrands estate) and 250 acres close to Upholland railway station (Pimbo estate).

The new population was to be drawn from Liverpool, principally from the boroughs of Bootle, Litherland, Crosby, Huyton-with-Roby and Kirkby.

As previously noted, the developments at Skelmersdale were of particular national interest because it was to be the first of a fresh wave of new towns following the lull that succeeded the building of the earlier postwar new towns. The report spoke of the need to think about minor details as well as major factors, if the town was to succeed. Consideration must be given to visual and social amenities as well as practical requirements.

Building density would be higher than in the Mark 1 new towns, comprising 60-75 dwellings per acre for most of the town and around 45 per acre for a smaller area of the town. Perhaps this was for economic rather than aesthetic reasons. We have already seen that the SDC was keen to experiment with construction techniques and perhaps also had an eye to economising on building costs.

With regard to the geological condition of the area, the report noted that sand extraction at Stormy Corner should be allowed to complete before any new development took place. It also noted that structural precautions might be necessary to avoid subsidence which might be caused by the presence of defunct mines throughout the development area. It considered that although all deep mines were flooded and presented little risk, shafts from shallow mines would need filling and capping.

With respect to the existing residential areas of the town the report noted that there were many scattered farmhouses which constituted, 'fine examples of 17th century vernacular style' (Wilson, ibid: 9). Unfortunately it seems that, although a few were saved, many more came under the bulldozer. Other housing was reputed to be in poor condition and new housing was dismissed as being, 'not very good to indifferent' (Wilson, ibid:9). This statement appears to demonstrate ambivalence on the part of the planners. On the one hand they verbally seem to hold to earlier new town ideals of quality and visual amenity, yet on the other they adopt a higher building density for most of the estates coupled with cheaper construction such as the pre-cast concrete method. In subsequent years the homes built by this method posed considerable problems of dampness and interior mould for tenants for many years until eventually extensive insulation procedures solved the difficulties.

Digmoor Hall farm, one of several 17ᵗʰ century farmhouses demolished to make way for the new town. It was sited in the area which is now Pimbo industrial estate. Photo courtesy of Harold Swift.

However, even at this early stage in the planning process, we can see that attention was directed in great detail to the whole life experience of the proposed population. We get an inkling of how incredibly difficult it is to design and construct a town, virtually from scratch. With hindsight it is easy to criticise the SDC planners, argue that they knew nothing about the area and its people but at every point the archives show meticulous planning and consultation. It is a sad fact that paper plans are transformed when put into practice; no one can plan for every eventuality or for unforeseen changes in the wider economic and political system.

Other eyes were also on developments in Skelmersdale. The council had been approached by the British Travel and Holiday Association who suggested the town might consider putting in some floral attractions for visitors. Presumably they thought that, like Letchworth, the new town would be a major tourist attraction, drawing crowds of the curious. In any event the council did consider setting up a tree nursery to service the visual requirements of the new town.

In October 1963, the Ormskirk Advertiser reported rumours that a compulsory purchase order served on Mr W. Gregson for land at Church Farm, offered a very low price in compensation (3.10.63). Earlier in the year, Mr Gregson had been in the news complaining about the noise of heavy plant outside his farmhouse as excavations for the new town got under way. Mr. Gregson's family had lived at New Church Farm for 70 years but now, he said that life was intolerable and even his donkeys, Nellie and Janey were fed up with the disturbance (Skelmersdale Reporter 25.6.63). All that now remains of New Church Farm is the name, given to the new town estate that now occupies its site. At the same time SDC proposed to build some prototype houses on land near Lime Grove in order to experiment with various construction methods. Wrangling over the cost of this land dragged on for many months with SDC persistently offering well below the amount deemed suitable by the council.

On 10th October, the SDC offices at the High Street, although only partially completed, were officially opened by Lord Derby. SDC suggested a meeting with Skelmersdale councillors to discuss their plans for the new town. Now these councillors were beginning to realise the full extent of the proposed developments and how they would impact on the old town centre at Sandy Lane. Serious worries were beginning to surface.

At regional level, Lancashire County Council's Education department was making plans for the educational needs of the new town, proposing a combined technical and academic college for 16-19 year olds. It estimated that 25-35% of the new population would be Roman Catholic, presumably taking into account the predominantly

Merseyside intake and the prevalence of Irish-Catholic families in traditional Liverpool communities.

Towards the end of October the fate of Pennylands was sealed with the council's decision to clear and redevelop it as soon as finance was available. The current residents were to be rehoused on the council's Church Farm estate. This planned redevelopment was separate from the SDC's plans for the New Church Farm estate in the area. However, the council obviously still felt in an excluded position as they had to wait for decisions from SDC before they could take action on their own behalf regarding redevelopments. Grants for improvements to homes in Witham Road were put on hold pending the forthcoming discussion with SDC, which was set for early November. Councillor Davies was quoted in the Ormskirk Advertiser (17.10.63), saying that the benefits of the new town would outweigh the sacrifices. He likened the developments to doctors' medicine, 'unpleasant but would do a lot of good.' Not everyone was convinced. CPRE was still voicing concerns about the green belt, provoking an assurance from Hugh Wilson that Ashurst Beacon would not be affected, that efforts would be made to preserve the old farmhouses where possible, and that existing trees and woodlands would be landscaped into the town. The words 'where possible' speak volumes here. In practice it meant that some old landmarks, such as Skelmersdale Hall (now the Toby Inn), Sutches farm (situated on the Holland Moor estate) and Postman's Cottage (in the middle of Acregate, Little Digmoor) would be preserved in the midst of the new town but others were summarily demolished, regardless of their age. In November the threatened closure of the railway line became a reality, cutting Skelmersdale off from railway transport. Residents would now have to travel to Ormskirk or Upholland to access rail links to Liverpool,Wigan and Manchester.

As plans for the new town went forward, the old town continued to be plagued by problems of maintenance and renewal. Many roads were reported to be in states of disrepair, and some streets were still unmade, despite the fast developing presence of the motor car. The sewerage system was overloaded and there were suspicions of possible subsidence damage due to the town's mining heritage (Ormskirk Advertiser 31.10.63). Alarmingly, the most urgent need for redevelopment was in the core of the old town. This officially reported position however, contrasts sharply with the perceptions of the town's residents. People living in the doomed Union and Penny Streets continued to protest against the Health Inspector's report, which labelled their homes as unfit for habitation. They seemed to see the report as a personal stigma, an attempt by the authorities to negate their efforts to keep a nice home, and a devaluation of their sense of community.

At a council meeting in November, Cllr. Caldwell sympathised with these residents but pointed out that in the wider picture, whole areas needed to be redeveloped. Situations like these must have been repeated nationwide as whole districts were demolished to provide new housing standards for our towns and cities. In addition, demolition was a preferred strategy from the perspective of town planners who had to think in terms of the need for new road systems to accommodate ever-increasing traffic.

This was the state of play as Skelmersdale prepared for its usual Christmas celebrations. One cannot help feeling that a sense of unknown doom seemed to be creeping over the town, rather than the enthusiastic vision that had manifested before the designation. With Christmas came the news that Callow Engineering was to be taken over by Western Holdings, a firm with branches in Manchester and the USA but a statement issued by the new board declared that the firm planned to continue to expand in Skelmersdale. The Boxing Day issue of the Ormskirk Advertiser reported the final sale of farm equipment at Mr Gregson's New Church Farm. Few farmers attended as they too would soon be losing their land to the SDC.

William Waterworth, a Dalton farmer recalls this time as one of heartbreak for local farmers, some of whose families had farmed Skelmersdale land for centuries. He reports seeing farmers in tears at the loss of their land and claims that despite compensation for their land, many farmers suffered financial problems due to their equipment being devalued because all the other farmers were also trying to sell theirs at the same time. Listening to these accounts it seems that once begun, the compulsory purchase of land proceeded very quickly. Mr Waterworth reports that some farmers were denied the opportunity to harvest their crops before the bulldozers appeared to break up their farms and states that although some went to new farms, others gave up farming for good and looked for other employment. He recalls the owners of Balcony Farm leaving to take up proprietorship of a garage in Upholland. Balcony Farm, another ancient building was left standing and later became an hotel. The hotel underwent several name changes and is currently known as the Lancashire Manor under Best Western ownership.

Some farmers tenaciously fought to stay on their land but eventually had to go. The owners of Feltons farm were the last to leave.

As the new year broke, Cllr. Margaret Green's name was put forward to the Minister of Housing, to fill the vacancy on the SDC board created by the death of Cllr. Farrimond.

The first stage of residential construction for the new town was due to begin in May 1964. Mindful of a possible shortage of builders once the new town construction got under way, Skelmersdale Council endeavoured to speed up the 150 new homes planned for Church Farm. Problems with some of the more dilapidated streets in the old town had been exacerbated by delays in clearance orders from central government, presumably pending plans for the new town, but in February compulsory purchase orders were confirmed on Penny and Union Streets. Although new homes on Church Farm were set aside for those who would be affected by the demolition, many protested that they would be unable to pay the rent of the new properties at £2.19s 0d. With the national average wage at just over £1000 p.a. in 1963, and probably much less for low paid workers, this sum represented a sizeable chunk of the weekly income. The Ormskirk Advertiser (13.3.64) reported that no information was then available as to the proposed use of the land once these streets had been cleared.

Perhaps as a result of the Penny and Union Streets tenants' protests, proposals were made in council chambers to make some of the planned dwellings at Church Farm in terraces to reduce costs and, consequently, rents. Meanwhile construction had already begun on two factories at Gillibrands to provide employment for the residents of the first new town estate.

Contrast of the old and the new. On the left the old potato works.
On the right the first factory building shines white.
Photo courtesy of William Waterworth.

Births in Skelmersdale for March that year totaled 12, a reminder of
just how small the indigenous population was when compared to the
proposed influx of 70,000 plus. Foreseeing a major increase,
Skelmersdale council was in negotiation with the North West
Electricity Board to set up a payment centre in the town. Formerly
people had to travel to Ormskirk to pay their bills but this would not
be feasible for a large population. Similarly, a new Crown post office
was planned for Skelmersdale, due to open in 1968 when the majority
of the planned new population would be in residence.

News broke that the top of Sandy Lane was to be closed to traffic
in two and a half years' time, although the reasons for this were not
stated. Applications for improvements to Sandy Lane were to be
turned down, (Ormskirk Advertiser 13.2.64.) indicating some
uncertainty as to the fate of the old town centre. A split was beginning
to form between those who embraced the new town and those who
wanted to protect the old. This was evident in the newly formed
Skelmersdale Association whose members argued over whether to

focus on protecting the old town, or on looking forward to the new town and visiting other new towns for inspiration. Suggestions made included pushing for a coach link to London and a monorail to connect Skelmersdale to Liverpool. Such ideas may seem fantastic but they demonstrate the futuristic vision that attached to the new town dream.

An issue of the Ormskirk Advertiser in March, advertised semi-detached private homes for sale in the 'Skelmersdale new town area;' presumably this was a desirable selling point. The homes referred to constituted the Neverstitch estate in School Lane and the properties were priced at £2450 for a 3 bed, £2575 for the same with garage.

Plans were coming together for service industries for the new town, including the licensing of new pubs, utilities such as water, gas and electricity and also for the provision of schools for the newcomers. Between 1965 and 1968, the Ministry of Education planned to provide one new secondary school, one Roman Catholic school and one Church of England primary school.

By April 1st. the building contract for the first new town homes was agreed with Unit Construction Company Ltd., a Liverpool firm. The contract was for 293 homes, 3 shops and 162 garages on New Church Farm at a cost of £868,000. Construction was to begin in June. Note the high proportion of garages to homes, reflecting the obsessive concerns of planners with the future of motor transport and the growing importance of the car as a family status symbol. The estate was planned to include space for every family to have a car with an additional 50% space to cater for visitors. The insistence of the new town planners on the coming importance of road transport has left Skelmersdale with an enduring legacy of trouble-free transport and parking facilities, of great advantage to residents and visitors alike (once they have become familiar with the town's roundabouts and its rather odd house numbering system!).

This contract represented only the first phase of the total 602 dwellings planned for New Church Farm. The first phase of building would use traditional methods but later phases would use industrialised techniques, probably following the results of the experimental properties SDC planned to build at Lime Grove. This explains the mixture of redbrick and concrete building on the early Skelmersdale estates. The first homes were due for completion by the end of the year. Suddenly castles in the air were promising to become concrete realities.

At this point, housing minister Sir Keith Joseph visited the SDC headquarters to view the plans and the area. This visit escalated bad feeling as the people of Skelmersdale, including its councillors, were not informed beforehand and no council representatives were invited.

By June then, plans were firmly laid for the first phase of the new town development. SDC finally acquired the site at Rose Crescent, where they planned to experiment with prototype houses for the later phases of building. This was only achieved at the cost of more bad feeling as they haggled for a long time over the price of this site and a paltry compensation of £5 only was paid to the occupiers of the garages currently on the site.

More than 40 firms were making enquiries about moving to the new town and a public meeting at Upholland Parish hall painted a glowing picture of the new town as a land where no skyscraper flats or air pollution would be permitted, contrasting it favourably to the town developments at Kirkby.

For some of the existing residents however, the prospect of the new town was alarming rather than reassuring. Many people felt that they were not being fully informed by SDC about what was going on. Perhaps these concerns were smoothed by the SDC's decision to set up a public meeting to discuss their plans for Digmoor, although, in fact, this simply meant they were moving on to plans for the next phase of construction.

As these developments unfolded and showed signs of coming together in major changes for the town, Skelmersdale did its best to carry on as usual. The council invited tenders for another 50 homes on Church Farm in early June and on the 18th June, the Skelmersdale Sunday School Walk and Flower Service at the parish church comprised 100 children. This tradition was the oldest annual procession in the town's history. Sadly, it occurs no longer.

In early June SDC announced proposals for a 436 acre development in Digmoor as phase 2 of the new town plan. They estimated an increase in the Digmoor population from 2000 to 18,300. The location was chosen for its proximity to the existing major A577 road to Wigan, which also connected to the new industrial estate at Gillibrands. SDC made the somewhat insensitive claim that the new development would unite the current scattered population of Digmoor. Such claims may have failed to convince the existing residents of the proposed benefits.

The Tawd Bridge area was to be excluded from the plan due to its proximity to the planned town centre. The Grimshaw Lane Inn was to be preserved, also the Hare and Hounds on Holland Moor but the axe was to fall on the Bowling Green. SDC also included a suggestion that experimental community facilities might be created at Grimshaw Delf. This suggestion was eventually put into practice with funding provided jointly by other organisations as well as SDC to form the Quarry Bank Association in the late 1960s.

The Bowling Green pub sited at the junction
of Daniels Lane and Spencers Lane.
Photo by kind permission of Harold Swift.

Age-related playgrounds were factored into the design for the Digmoor estates with larger game pitches on the peripheries. Playing fields were designated for land between Sutches Farm and Chequer Lane. Sutches Farm itself was retained by the development corporation and for many years was used as a community centre for local residents.

88

On the wider front, SDC was getting down to practical details including inviting tenders for the provision of 'paper dustbins' for refuse collection in the new town. Roads were being laid, in preparation for the new businesses and residents. The uprooting of a 50 year old sycamore to make way for a new town road was reported by the Ormskirk Advertiser (18.6.64). Did this throw doubt on the SDC pledge to preserve Skelmersdale's traditional landscape? Perhaps not as the tree was replanted at one of the new factory sites.

Two new councillors are admitted to the board of Skelmersdale Development Corporation: Cllr.Bamforth (Upholland) and Cllr

Davies (Skelmersdale). The appointment of an Upholland councillor perhaps reflects the inclusion of Upholland in the new town status. Also pictured are Chairman of the board, A.J. Kentish Barnes and board member Brian Park. Photograph: Skelmersdale Reporter 18.6.64

On 24th June 1964, an official ceremony was held to celebrate the laying of the first brick of the new town and to look forward to its prospects. Alderman Louis Caplan, Lord Mayor of Liverpool, spoke of the new town as being a self-contained community, with its own industries, traditions and culture. He said it would develop its own character, being so much more than a slum clearance project. The fact that the ceremony was conducted by a Liverpool official rather than someone from Lancashire, perhaps says something about the nature of the character the town was expected to assume. The same week, the head of Callow Engineering flew to Russia to negotiate a half million pound contract for its Skelmersdale factory, a far cry from the small traditional industries of the town. This major deal seemed an omen of good fortune, presaging a bright new future for Skelmersdale.

In earlier chapters we have followed the history of the little village of Skelmersdale through its burgeoning growth as a mining town and subsequent decay as its lifeblood, the mines, fell into decline. At the end of this book we see Skelmersdale for the second time in its history, about to experience the rush of energy and enthusiasm involved in rebuilding itself. Hopes were high that the town would rise like a phoenix from the ashes, yet many feared the destruction of their traditions and the coming influx of strangers.

Bulldozers move in. Photograph by kind permission of David Ball. www.glassball.org.uk

91

References
Bagley, J.J. (1976) *A History of Lancashire.* Henley on Thames: Darwen Finlayson Ltd.

Baines, E. (1870) *The History of the County Palatine and Duchy of Lancaster Vol.2* (revised ed.). London: Routledge.

Boxshall, J. (1997) *Every Home Should Have One.* London: Good Housekeeping.

Bruce, J. (Ed.) (1999) *Three Early Modern Utopias.* London: Oxford University Press.

Cuckson, M. (1997) *The Light of Other Days:Recollections of a Skelmersdale Childhood.* Ormskirk: Ormskirk Book and Art Shop.

Ekwall, E. (1972) *The Place Names of Lancashire.* Lancashire: EP Publishing.

Godfrey, A. (2001) *Old Ordnance Survey Maps: Skelmersdale 1907.* Consett: Alan Godfrey Maps.

Hall, P. & Ward, C. (1998) *Sociable Cities: The Legacy of Ebenezer Howard.* UK: John Wiley & Sons.

Harris, S.A. (1956) *The Development of Gas Supply in North Merseyside 1815 – 1949.* Liverpool: North Western Gas Board.

Hodges,M. (undatedc.1996) *Memories of Skelmersdale in the 1920s and 1930s.* Skelmersdale: Hodges, M.

Howard, E. (1965 edn.) *Garden Cities of Tomorrow.* London: Faber & Faber.

Kirkby, J. (1745) *The Capacity and Extent of the Human Understanding Exemplified in the Extraordinary Case of Automathes, A Young Nobleman.* London: R.Manby & H. Shute Cox. Eighteenth Century Collections Online:http://o-find.galegroup.com.library.edgehill.ac.uk [accessed 15.10.2007].

Malia, S. (undated c.2000) *Ormskirk and District Football: The Early Years 1880-1914.* Self-published chapbook

Mills, D. (1976) *The Place Names of Lancashire.* London: B.T. Batsford Ltd.

Molyneux, J. (1981) *Population Movements in Nineteenth Century Lancashire: Impact and Reality – the Case of Skelmersdale.*

Dissertation for degree of B.A. in History, submitted to Lancaster University (Edge Hill College of Higher Education).

More, T. (1516) *Utopia,* in Bruce, S. (ed.) (1999), *Three Early Modern Utopias.* UK: Oxford University Press.

Mumford, L. (1945) 'The Garden City Idea and Modern Planning,' in Howard, E. (1946) *Garden Cities of Tomorrow.* London: Faber & Faber, pp29-40.

Orr, G. (2005) *The History of Skelmersdale from the Domesday Book to the 20th Century.* Skelmersdale: G.Orr.

Osborn, F.J.(1945) 'Preface to Garden Cities of Tomorrow,' in Howard, E.(1965 edn.) *Garden Cities of Tomorrow.* London: Faber&Faber.

Osborn, F.J. & Whittick, A. (1969) *The New Towns: The Answer to Megalopolis.* London: Leonard Hill.

Padfield, H. (1986) *The Story of Ormskirk.* Preston: Carnegie Press.

Page, W. (ed.) (1907) *The Victorian History of the Counties of England, Vol.3 Victorian History of the County of Lancaster.* UK: A.Constable & Co.

Sands, Rev. N. (1970) *The Skelmersdale Story.* Ormskirk: Ormskirk Advertiser Group.

Skelmersdale Heritage Society (2007) *Colliery Walks.* Skelmersdale: Skelmersdale Heritage Society.

Tait, D.B. (1979) *Skelmersdale: Class Formation in a New Town.* PhD thesis submitted to Faculty of Economics, London School of Economics. London: Hodder & Stoughton, University Press of Liverpool.

Ward, S. (1994) *Planning and Urban Change.* London: Leonard Hill

Yates, T. (undated, c.1976) *My Memories.* Skelmersdale: self-published, accessed Skelmersdale Library.

Government Acts and reports.

Barlow Report (1940) *The Royal Commission on the Distribution of the Industrial Population.* London: HMSO.

Buchanan Report (1963) *Traffic in Towns.* London: HMSO.

South West Lancashire Joint Town Planning Advisory Committee (1930) *The Future Development of South West Lancashire.* London: University Press of Liverpool/Hodder & Stoughton.

Town and Country (amendment) Planning Act 1972. London: HMSO.

Wilson, L. H. (1963) *Skelmersdale New Town: Interim Report on Planning Proposals* Skelmersdale: Skelmersdale Development Corporation.

Newspapers, miscellaneous publications and presentations.
Newspapers:
Guardian 17.9.60:12 'New Town Named For Merseyside.'
Ormskirk Advertiser 1930-1964.
Skelmersdale Reporter 1963-64.
Sunday Times, 24.12.95. 'Bathed In Sunlight.'
Sunday Times, 27.7.03 'Bye Bye New Town, Hello Garden City.'

Presentations:
Howell, M. (2010) *The History of Skelmersdale.* Presentation given in Skelmersdale library 18.3.10 for West Lancashire Libraries.